Praise for *Buying Trances*

"The genius of Joe Vitale has never shone brighter. This thoroughly documented and easy-to-read tome on Buying Trances is the first of its kind. Vitale gives you the keys to their minds. All you have to do is turn the keys. They said yes to you long before you said a word . . . and were begging to buy from you shortly after you uttered your first sentences. *Buying Trances* is an exciting ride to the edge of the mind. It's Joe's finest work to date."

—Kevin Hogan, Author of *The Psychology of Persuasion* and *Covert Persuasion*

"I absolutely refuse to endorse this book at all because of the chapter on the all-time best trance inducer. I feel it is dangerous and irresponsible to expose this information. Joe, what were you thinking? If I were going to endorse this book, I might say something like: This book maps marketing's final frontier—the customer's mind—and exposes their Buying Trance. Frankly, this may be the smartest marketing book ever written, yet that chapter makes it the most dangerous book on the planet in the wrong hands. Proceed with caution."

—Dave Lakhani, Author of *Persuasion: The Art of Getting What You Want*

"As with all of Joe's books, there are magical secrets dealt out like a mad Vegas poker dealer on every page. Not only will you learn to put people into Buying Trances with this book, the act of reading it will put *you* in one and force you to master it."

—Mark Joyner, Author of *The Irresistible Offer*

"Joe Vitale's expertise in hypnotic marketing, combined with his extensive research, challenges the reader on many different levels. He forces you to delve deeper into the benefits of creating a buying atmosphere and a trancelike desire on the part of your prospect. I found this an absolutely fascinating book."

—Joseph Sugarman, President,
BluBlocker Corporation

"*Buying Trances* is not your run-of-the-mill marketing book. It's an exceptionally well-written, well-thought-out, high-level work that gives the reader unique insights into how to capture his/her prospect's attention. Cutting-edge stuff that is a must for every serious marketer to absorb and implement."

—Robert Ringer, Author of *To Be or Not to Be Intimidated?*

"Once again Joe Vitale has written another masterpiece but this surely must be his finest work! Joe's understanding of how and why people think and act like they do is remarkable. By unscrambling complex ideas and explaining them in simple language he reveals how to fashion messages that will turn people into compulsive buyers of our products and services. Now we can take control and create the Buying Trance. It's a totally refreshing and very effective approach to hugely profitable sales and marketing!"

—Winston Marsh, Veteran
Australian Marketer

"Dr. Joe Vitale has written a very informative, entertaining, and dangerous book. By revealing the deep, secret workings of the buyer's mind, he makes it all too easy to analyze anyone's current mental and emotional state, and use that knowledge to put prospects in a helpless Buying Trance. Whether you're selling or buying, buy this book for your own protection."

—Pat O'Bryan, Director, Milagro
Research Institute,
www.patobryan.com

"*Buying Trances* isn't about controlling or manipulating customers. It's about how to get your sales message heard by the people most likely to act on it. When your offer matches your market's desires, you will get their attention.

However, you'll quickly see that Joe Vitale believes most people in sales and marketing are stuck in a selling trance. Without a change in focus, you'll alienate your customers and the competition will eat you alive.

The concepts presented in this book, once applied, will make it easier for you to truly reach your customers—and make the sale. I highly recommend this book to anyone in sales or marketing. Not only is this a well-written, intelligent book, it's a fun read, too."

—Bill Hibbler,
www.ecommerceconfidential.com

"If you want to understand how to match what your customer is thinking about and lead them to want to buy from you, this is a must-have book. I couldn't put it down! Whether I'm writing a sales letter, an e-mail to my list, or a blog post, this book has given me quick and easy ways to make sure I'm reaching my prospects in their trance and bringing them into mine. As advertising overload saturates your customers' attention, tapping into the power of Buying Trances not only will be sharp marketing, but it may well become essential for your business's survival."

—Craig Perrine,
www.maverickmarketer.com

Buying Trances

Buying Trances

A New Psychology
of Sales
and Marketing

Joe Vitale

John Wiley & Sons, Inc.

Published by John Wiley & Sons, Inc., Hoboken, New Jersey.
Published simultaneously in Canada.

Wiley Bicentennial Logo: Richard J. Pacifico

For general information on our other products and services or for technical support, please contact our Customer Care Department within the U.S. at (800) 762-2974, outside the United States at (317) 572-3993 or fax (317) 572-4002.

Wiley also publishes its books in a variety of electronic formats. Some content that appears in print may not be available in electronic books. For more information about Wiley products, visit our web site at www.wiley.com.

Library of Congress Cataloging-in-Publication Data:

Vitale, Joe, 1953–
    Buying trances : a new psychology of sales and marketing / Joe Vitale.
      p. cm.
    Includes bibliographical references and index.
    ISBN 978-0-470-09519-5 (cloth)
    1. Selling—Psychological aspects.   2. Marketing—Psychological aspects.   I. Title.
    HF5438.8.P75V58   2007
    658.8001'9—dc22

                              2006031241

Printed in the United States of America.

10 9 8 7 6 5 4 3 2 1

To Roy Garn and Milton Erickson

Nothing more directly challenges status quo marketing research than the emerging scientific consensus that almost all mental activity isn't fully conscious.

—Dan Hill, *Body of Truth: Leveraging What Consumers Can't or Won't Say*, 2003

Ideas which have the greatest suggestive power are those presented to us by the actions of other persons. The second most effective class is probably the ideas suggested by the words of our companions. Advertisements that are seen frequently are difficult to distinguish in their force from ideas which are secured from the words of our friends. Advertising thus becomes a great social illusion.

—Walter Dill Scott, *The Psychology of Advertising*, 1908

Contents

Foreword

Buying Trances.
    Three for $1,000?

Some trances are absolutely amazing.

They can take you deep inside the most passionate of places or move you to the peaks of peaceful calm; still others can bring you the power and perseverance you might want to be the best at what you do.

Trances.

Three for $1,000 could be a bargain.

Trances fascinate.

The moments before you fall into slumber are called the *hypnogogic* state. The moments you are waking up, unsure of whether you are walking around or still in bed, only to be assured you are still in bed, are the *hypnopompic* state.

Every day you and I experience these two states. In an average person's day there is no time that we are more susceptible to suggestion, which is why I stopped listening to the radio in bed two decades ago.

Joe Vitale calls himself a hypnotic marketer, an appropriate title for what he does.

Hypnotic writing?

Joe coined that phrase and I love it.

Sounds absurd when you first hear it, doesn't it?

Isn't hypnosis where you stare at a watch and go to sleep

and hold your arm out for an hour while someone gives you suggestions, after which you remember nothing?

Certainly that could be one kind of trance or one trancelike state (not a great state for buying products and services, though).

Hypnotic writing.

Lewis Carroll wrote perhaps the single most powerful piece of hypnotic writing in history: *Alice's Adventures In Wonderland*.

Have you read that recently?

May I suggest what the power of the mind can do . . . and the power of a trance? Please grab a copy off your bookshelf and simply read the first 15 pages or so.

Alice sees a rabbit. He carries a watch. He goes into a hole. She follows.

She gets tall and small.

She gets wide and thin.

She has adventures that she never wanted but would have a story to tell for life. I promise you—read the first 15 pages or so and you will be in one of the most surprisingly focused trances you'll ever experience.

Someone can tap you on the shoulder and call your name, but you won't be aware that anyone is there because you are in Lewis Carroll's world, and will come out of it only when *he* says it's time.

And you can learn to write in such a way that causes people to *stop*, forget what they were just thinking, turn off the lights, put an X on the piece of paper in front of them, hold it up to the moonlight, hear the crickets, and see the shadows extending across the landscape.

And it's important to get people to *stop* what they were doing and bring them to your landscape after you've been in their minds, because you can't sell to them if you don't turn off the trance they're in and bring them into yours.

The recent *War of the Worlds* movie with Tom Cruise isn't scary at all unless you have watched the first 15 minutes during which you see that everything is normal in New York. Dad plays catch with his irritable teenage son and there is tension between them as there is in anyone's family; the little girl . . . well, she almost gets lost in Dad's house because it's such a mess. Then *stop* . . . the earth opens up.

And that is where you are taken from your trance, normal life in New York, and put into Steven Spielberg's trance, the invasion of the planet.

There are two fundamental ways to move people out of their trances.

One is to get into their landscape, show them you understand their world, show them you can live in their world, and show them you empathize with their problems (you could write the book), and then, once you have them captured, *boom*! you invade the earth.

The other is to simply cause brief single-second confusion for the person.

You do this by accident every day. You are walking to the den or the living room and you forget why. You look around. People stare at you and you look silly because you can't even venture a guess as to why you left that other room.

Of course, you go back to your room or office, sit down, and are instantly back in your world—you remember exactly what you were going out for.

But what got you sidetracked?

Maybe someone's tie wasn't straight.

Maybe you saw a paycheck on someone's desk or a magazine lying on the floor. Whatever it was, you didn't in any way anticipate it and it took you from your trance to their trance.

In hypnosis it's called a *confusion technique*.

My research shows that if you confuse people for just a moment and bring them into your trance, you can capture their minds. But once they are confused you have only seconds to capture their attention, or all is lost and they will return to their own trances.

Remember Alice in Wonderland?

Exactly.

It seems like such a long time ago!

Why?

Because since we talked about Alice, we've been invaded by aliens and seen someone's goofy tie and someone's paycheck. We've done a lot of traveling in our minds. Walking from room to room, talking to kids—all that stuff gives the brain the illusion of time, making it seem long ago that we were talking about Alice, but it wasn't. It was only five minutes. It seems like hours, and conversely, sometimes in trances hours seem like minutes.

But I'll leave all of that for Joe Vitale.

Buying Trances will help you understand how people think so you can help people buy—from you.

—Kevin Hogan
www.kevinhogan.com

Eagan, Minnesota
September 2006

Acknowledgments

An author writes a book alone but is heavily influenced by family, friends, peers, strangers, and other authors. I want to thank everyone involved in creating this book. Nerissa, my love, is my main support person, domestic partner, and best friend. Matt Holt and my friends at John Wiley & Sons are terrific people to know and work with. Blair Warren and David Deutsch are best friends and lovers of books. Suzanne Burns is my key assistant and publicist, and a positive influence in my life. Kevin Hogan helped me become a better hypnotist. David Garfinkel, Mark Joyner, and everyone in my mastermind group, including Jillian Coleman-Wheeler, Cindy Cashman, Craig Perrine, Pat O'Bryan, Bill Hibbler, and Nerissa Oden, supported me in this project. Thank you, one and all.

Author's Strange Introduction

Last night, friends came over for dinner. Victoria, a writer who publishes a local newspaper, asked what I was working on these days.

"I've got several books I'm writing or promoting at any one time," I replied. "There's also my fitness program, my membership program, the nutritional supplement formulas I've invested in and am promoting, my travels, my clients, and lots more."

"What's the book you're writing currently?" she asked.

"It's called *Buying Trances*," I answered. "It's about a new psychology of sales and marketing."

Her eyes lit up with interest. Her husband, sitting beside her, didn't say anything. Victoria, looking captivated, asked the obvious next question: "What's a buying trance?"

I paused to collect my thoughts and then said, "Everyone is already in a trance. People are thinking about their problems and their dreams. They aren't thinking about you and what you want to sell to them. This isn't negative. They are simply preoccupied with their lives. In order to make a sale today, you have to meet them in their current trances, then guide them to what you want them to focus on, which is your product or service. If you don't meet them where they are in their heads, they'll never hear you, let alone buy from you."

"So you need to find out what's on their minds before you try to persuade them?" Victoria offered.

That, in essence, is the definition of a Buying Trance. It's meeting people *where they are* before you take them *where you want them to go*. It's the difference between a sideshow barker yelling for people to "Step right up!" and buy his product and you treating them as friends you care about and want to help. The former is going for a quick sale; the latter is going for a profitable long-term relationship. This book is about the latter.

Now, stop and reflect on the unspoken elements of the preceding story.

Victoria is a newspaper publisher. She is naturally interested in books and words. Her question came from her existing "trance" and my answer spoke to that existing mental state. Had I not addressed her question, or had I instead talked about my nutritional supplement company, she might have lost interest, fogged out, and never heard a word I said.

And note that her husband, sitting at the same table, didn't show much interest in the conversation. He was polite and looked attentive, but he was not involved. He's into bike riding, video production, and health. Had I talked about any of those subjects, he would have leaned forward and asked a lot of questions. He wasn't in a Buying Trance. His wife was.

Your readers, prospects, customers, and clients are all like this. When your sales and marketing reaches them, it arrives when *they aren't there*. They may be present physically, but not mentally. In their minds, they are preoccupied with their lives. You may be granted about *10 seconds* to make your case. If you don't connect to their trance or bring them out of their trance in those precious 10 seconds, the chances for a sale are next to none.

This book is intended to help you discover how to better communicate with people, so that your sales messages are heard and acted on. You'll find that little things will make a difference. For example, look at the title of this introduction. By adding the word *strange*, I made a simple introduction much more, well, hypnotic. While most readers skip introductions to get right to the meat of a book, chances are very high you stopped to read this one, all because of an added word that broke your existing trance.

This is where the world of the Buying Trance begins.

As you proceed through this book, here are a few ideas and questions to allow into your awareness:

- What would your sales and marketing be like if you found yourself understanding Buying Trances and naturally using them in your business?

- You don't have to use the Buying Trance right away; it's only important that you are open to the idea of using it soon.

- What would it be like if you allowed your use of the Buying Trance to evolve naturally, easily, and quickly?

- If you were to understand how powerful the Buying Trance is, how much more would you enjoy reading this book?

- You might notice how a single word can define your focus, as well as that of your prospect, customer, or client.

- Just pretend for a moment that you're the kind of person who can easily master this information and become good at using the Buying Trance.

- I know you are wondering what all of this has to do with sales and marketing, and that's a good thing to wonder.

- When you find yourself using the Buying Trance naturally, will you be really surprised or just delighted?

Whatever your answers or thoughts at this point in time, just pretend that all of it is moving you in the direction of more sales, more fun, and longer and more profitable relationships.

As you relax into your chair, alert yet calm, let's begin.

—Dr. Joe Vitale
www.mrfire.com

Austin, Texas
September 2006

Buying Trances

GOT TRANCE?

Are you reading these words right now?

That question isn't as obvious as it may first appear.

You may be looking at this page, but chances are very good that a part of your mind is wandering, or is about to wander. You might be thinking about your next meal, next appointment, next book, next sale, or any number of things.

In essence, you are in a trance. Your mind is focused on these words, but if I write the wrong word or phrase and activate a new mental process within you, your mind may run off in a new direction. You may put this book down and not complete this page, let alone this chapter. It all depends on what I trigger within you.

Now, stop and consider:

As you read the preceding paragraphs, did your mind in fact wander off?

When I mentioned your next meal, did your stomach begin to grumble?

When I mentioned your next appointment, did you glance at your watch?

When I mentioned your next book, did you think of other books you want to read?

I've been very careful not to suggest anything outright stimulating. If I did, your mind *would* wander off. As it is, even with the innocent triggers I've listed, I bet your mind still left the page at least a few times.

This little exercise should give you a small sense of what your own prospective customers are going through as you talk to them or ask them to read a letter or e-mail from you or visit your web site. They are preoccupied. They are thinking of themselves and their interests.

They are in a trance.

YOUR WAKING TRANCE

The trance people are in isn't a *somnambulistic* one, during which they are deep asleep but conscious of spoken words. It's more of a *waking trance*, during which they are alert and aware; their eyes are open, but their minds are focused on something other than what is right in front of them.

The term *waking trance* was coined in 1924 by Wesley Wells. In my recent book, *Hypnotic Writing*, I defined it this way: "A waking trance is a concentration of attention. You are focused on something before you, to the exclusion of virtually all else. Whenever you read a fascinating book, you are engaged in a mild trance. Because your eyes are open, this state is called a *waking trance*."

Everyday waking trances are common. They help us get through the day. When you have a long drive to make, so-called highway hypnosis slides in and you safely drive, but you aren't totally aware of time. When you read a good book, your mind focuses on it and, at least for a while, you forget the world around you. When you are in a conversation with someone, you are somewhat focused on them but mostly focused on your next words or point.

You've experienced those trance states. However, few

people realize that most of their life is spent in a trance of one form or another.

- Stephen Wolinsky writes, in *Trances People Live*: "Trances are often a necessary means of surviving and negotiating the physical universe. They are like tunnels you walk through in order to maneuver and focus in the world."
- Stephen Gilligan writes, in *Therapeutic Trances*: "Trance experiences are not divorced from a person's normal patterns of functioning."
- Roger Straus writes, in *Creative Self-Hypnosis*: "We are all walking around in something like a trance, sleepwalking through our lives, following what amounts to a set of 'post-natal suggestions' to be a certain kind of person and to think and behave in a certain way."
- According to Ronald Havens' *The Wisdom of Milton H. Erickson*, the legendary hypnotherapist once said, "Trance is a common experience. A football fan watching a game on TV is awake to the game but is not awake to his body sitting in the chair or his wife calling him to dinner."

Almost no one in business understands that unless you merge with and lead the existing trance of your customers, your chances for a sale are slim to none. This book is about awakening you from the trance most businesspeople are in and putting you into a new trance: one in which you are in control.

This may be confusing. But as I pointed out in my book *The Attractor Factor*, confusion is that wonderful state right before clarity. Confusion itself is a trance. Clarity is another one.

This book is about awakening from trances.

A NEW PSYCHOLOGY

A trance is defined as any condition where the focus of attention is narrowed. This is why so many traditionally trained hypnotists ask their subjects or patients to focus on something specific, such as a candle flame, a point on the wall, a swinging watch, or even just a finger. This focusing of attention, a characteristic of the trance state, is a way to actually induce a trance.

You can do this with words spoken or written. My book *Hypnotic Writing* explains how to use words to seduce people into paying attention and then paying for your product or service. Words can lead people into a waking trance state. For the purposes of this book, we will use words to lead people into what I call a Buying Trance.

The Buying Trance is a focusing of attention on what a person will get from your product or service. As long as you focus their attention on *their* needs, you can keep people in a Buying Trance. But this is easier said than done. The average person in business is focused on his or her own needs: to make a sale. She or he is stuck in a *selling* trance, which doesn't put anyone in a *buying* trance. The difference is dramatic.

I'm calling this procedure a new psychology of sales and marketing because it is a breakthrough in the psychology of selling. Modern psychology hasn't been around more than 150 years, according to James Goodwin in his book, *A History of Modern Psychology*. Business psychology is even younger.

The first popular psychologist in the business arena was Walter Dill Scott. He wrote many books, beginning in 1903 with *The Theory of Advertising*. Scott said consumers were not rational decision makers and could be influenced by suggestion and emotion. He scratched the surface of how to begin a Buying Trance, though he never used that term. Still, Scott was strongly influenced in his view of suggestion by the work of H. Bernheim on hypnosis, especially by the 1889 book, *Suggestive Therapeutics: A Treatise on the Nature and Uses of Hypnotism*.

My own work in sales and marketing has been influenced by hypnotists and hypnotherapists. Knowing how the human mind works better enables any marketer to produce more focused, memorable, and practical messages. Since the average person is bombarded with an estimated two to three thousand selling messages per day, most of which they never remember or remember incorrectly, business needs a better way to grab and hold attention. Using principles of hypnosis in selling can help create that Buying Trance, where your chances of making more sales increase.

In this book you'll learn how to create a Buying Trance that serves your customers. You won't be able to control or manipulate them, but you will be able to get your message heard by your target audience. When your message is a match to what your audience needs or wants, you'll find that they perk up and focus on you, which is the essence of waking hypnosis.

Keep an open mind. You're about to discover a breakthrough—a powerful new tool for increasing your results in all your sales and marketing.

WHY YOU NEED THIS

Why is knowing how to put people into a Buying Trance important?

The answer should be obvious: You've got competition. Some of it is from unscrupulous advertisers and marketers; some of it is from people who aren't even in your business; and lots of it is from businesses that are simply cluttering the marketplace with their messages, most of which fall on deaf ears.

I tried to get a firm number as to how many sales and marketing messages the average person hears or sees in one day. The numbers I found are conflicting, but seem to average about 3,000 per day. For example:

- Tony Rubleski, in his book, *Mind Capture*, says we are hit by 1,500 messages per day.

- Mike Adams, in his booklet, *The Real Safety Guide to Protecting Against Advertisers, Marketers and Big Business Propaganda*, says we are exposed to more than 3,000 commercial messages a day.

Some of my other research revealed the following:

The average person today is exposed to never-ending deluge of 1,700 marketing messages during a single 24-hour period. Look around you; we marketers have pasted integrated, injected, and/or overlaid advertising in any possible place imaginable! Case in point: NBC will start to digitally insert commercial "billboards" into advertising content to be broadcast during the Winter Olympics—in essence a commercial within a commercial.

www.intelective.com/online-internet-marketing-firm.pdf

According to a recent consumer expenditure survey, households spend $4 trillion per year. It's estimated that $236 billion will be spent this year in the United States on print, radio, online, and broadcast advertising to get a piece of this market. The result is sensory bombardment. It is also estimated that each American is exposed to well over 2,500 advertising messages per day, and that children see over 50,000 TV commercials a year. In our view, as many as one-quarter of all these ads are deliberately deceptive. Increasingly, the family of businesses that advertise is not one you should be proud to be associated with.

www.nolo.com/product.cfm/objectID/5E5BFB9E-A33A-43DB-9D162A6460AA646A/sampleChapter/5/111/277/

An effective marketing plan can help you cut through the clutter. Did you know the average adult is hit with 3,000 marketing messages per day? How do you know your message is getting through and, more importantly, your message is getting to the right person? A marketing plan will let you answer these questions with confidence an a sense of satisfaction.

www.fairfaxcountyeda.org/tw_potomac.htm

Advertising has long been a sort of black art with a murky ROI [return on investment] and for a simple reason. Clients rarely know for sure who sees their ads, let alone whether the ads influence anyone. Even though companies spend a third of a trillion dollars a year on advertising, those ads often end up being irrelevant to the people who see them. On average, Americans are subject to some 3,000 essentially random pitches per day. Two-thirds of people surveyed in a Yankelovich Partners study said they feel "constantly bombarded" by ads, and 59% said the ads they see have little or no relevance to them. No wonder so many people dislike and ignore advertising, and so many business owners feel gun-shy about investing in serious campaigns.

www.inc.com/magazine/20050801/future-of-advertising.html

Your potential customers are being hammered with marketing messages through the day and night. One statistic I heard was that we now experience *3,000 different marketing messages in an average day* (from slogans, jingles, spam, e-mails, billboards, direct mail, image advertising, branding campaigns, etc.)

http://advertising.ducttapemarketing
.com/2006/02/index.html

Consumers and business-to-business clients have distinct preferences in how they prefer their communications. And when people are bombarded with over 3,000 messages daily, yours can easily get lost in a sea of messaging in a variety of channels.

www.marketingprofs.com/6/fogel6.asp

Believe it or not, The Million Dollar Homepage is sold out. Most of the ads are tiny (the minimum was a 100-pixel ad), so the result is a visual cacophony of banner ads like none you have ever seen. If it's true that the average American is exposed to 5,000 advertising and promotional messages per day, you can get your minimum daily requirement just by going to The Million Dollar Homepage every morning.

www.tompeters.com/blogs/main/marketing/index.php

As should be painfully clear by now, the number of messages in the marketplace is overwhelming. Although you may have a product or service worth gold, your target audience may never hear about it unless you utilize some new tools, such as the Buying Trance.

THERE'S GOT TO BE A BETTER WAY!

Even if you disregard the number of marketing messages that are shot at people all day long, there's also the reality that people are tuning out those messages. They're not listening to you!

Your audience is fed up with marketing. They've had it. They'll do almost anything to turn off the advertising or block it. To prove this, here are some facts from the Yankelovich Partners research on advertising and marketing:

- Some 60 percent of consumers have a much more negative opinion of marketing and advertising now than they did a few years ago.
- Just 61 percent feel the amount of marketing and advertising is out of control.
- About 65 percent feel constantly bombarded with too much marketing and advertising.
- Of consumers polled, 53 percent said that spam had turned them off to all forms of marketing and advertising.
- Of consumers polled, 36 percent said that the shopping experience is less enjoyable because of pressure to buy.
- About 53 percent said that, for the most part, marketing and advertising do not help them shop better.
- Some 59 percent feel that most marketing and advertising has very little relevance to them.
- Just 64 percent are concerned about practices and motives of marketers and advertisers.
- About 61 percent feel that marketers and advertisers don't treat consumers with respect.
- Some 65 percent think there should be more limits and regulations on marketing and advertising.

- About 69 percent are interested in products and services that would help them skip or block marketing.

- Just 33 percent would be willing to have a slightly lower standard of living to live in a society without marketing and advertising.

Those statistics should jar you. Have no fear, though: There is a better way to reach your customers and clients—it's called the Buying Trance.

EXPECT TO LEARN

A few weeks ago I was stuck at the San Jose, California, airport, waiting for the airline to find a safe plane to get me back home to Texas.

I sat there for nine hours.

While a lot of other passengers kicked and moaned and otherwise had fits, I and maybe a dozen others went with the flow. I used the downtime to write, read, and relax. One of the books I had stuffed into my bag was good for my mind, was a delight to read, taught me a few things, and prompted me to write this section.

According to Richard Restak, in *The New Brain: How the Modern Age Is Rewiring Your Mind*, your brain is plastic. You can teach your brain new tricks, skills, languages, and more with repetition, intention, awareness, and patience. He says there is a 10-year rule stating that virtually anyone can become a genius—or at least a superior performer—in a niche if they apply themselves in that area for a decade.

As I think about how I became an author, then a copywriter, then a publicist, then a speaker, and then an Internet marketer, I can see I spent decades learning those subjects and honing my skills. I read books, studied authors, bought courses, and invested in weekend seminars and trainings. I put myself through a relentless and disciplined self-study and home-study quest to learn and grow.

I still do this today. I was stuck at the San Jose airport because I had flown there to attend a weekend seminar. And, just the weekend before, I held the world's first Manifestation Weekend (www.beyondmanifestation.com), where already successful people came from all over the world to see how much more successful they could be.

The point: If you want to become a better salesperson, or marketer, or copywriter, or author, or speaker, or anything else, you should expect to invest time, energy, and money to learn the craft. You should expect it to take longer than a weekend. You can *start* the process in a moment, with a decision, and you can see progress very quickly, but mastery will take a little longer.

Maybe even 10 years.

But if you don't *start now*, where will you be in 10 years?

OPEN YOUR MIND-SET

Carol Dweck, in her wonderful book, *Mindset: The New Psychology of Success*, explains that there are two perspectives to growth in your life: a fixed mind-set and a growth mind-set.

The fixed mind-set is where you decide you cannot learn anything new in an area, no matter how much you try. Your ability is *fixed*.

The growth mind-set, in contrast, is one whereby you feel you can learn with enough energy, focus, time, and commitment. Your ability is flexible. You are able to *grow*.

When I read Dweck's book, I thought about the world of marketing. In that area, I have a growth mind-set. I feel I can learn new things with guidance and effort. In other areas I had a fixed mind-set. When it came to performing magic for others, for example, I felt my skills were fixed at a poor level. Even though I love magic, am on the board of the local magic group, and am a lifetime member of a famous magic organization, I felt my performing skills were fixed. After reading Dweck's book, I decided that was not true. I awoke to the fact that I can learn anything, even how to perform magic, if I focus on it and work at it. Today, I perform magic for anyone who asks, and sometimes for those who don't ask.

The same concept holds true in my professional career when it came to direct selling. At one point I had a fixed mind-set about my ability to deal with powerful people. I was intimated by them. As I changed that old mind-set to a growth mind-set, I've been able to deal with the offices of such tycoons as Donald Trump, Sir Richard Branson, and Kenneth Feld.

As you read this book, I encourage you to come from a growth mind-set. Although some of the concepts may be new to you, that doesn't mean you can't implement them. It simply means they are new to you. Nothing more.

When I first started to learn how to play the harmonica, I thought it was impossible to get air through a single tiny hole. Anyone can blow air through *all* those holes, but narrowing the air flow to a single controlled note seemed impossible. I almost gave up numerous times. I felt my skills were fixed: I was not a harmonica player. It was not in the cards.

But I persisted. Over time, I gained the ability to control my air and direct my breathing. Today I can play virtually anything on the harmonica, from blues to classical music. Today it seems natural. In the beginning, however, it seemed impossible.

When I first began to learn new languages, such as Italian and Hawaiian, I found the new words to be staggeringly difficult. I felt I would never retrain my mind. But by adopting a growth mind-set, by realizing I could learn anything with time and persistence, I was able to learn conversational Italian in time for a trip to Italy, and I'm still learning Hawaiian.

Advises Dweck, "Picture your brain forming new connections as you meet the challenge and learn. Keep on going."

As you practice what you'll learn here, the entire process will become easier and easier. And then, one day, it will be second nature to you. It all begins with your mind-set.

Steve Andreas, in his two-volume work, *Six Blind Elephants*, says, "It is one thing to realize that the beginning stages of learning are often inevitably difficult and uncomfortable. It is quite another to use that discomfort as a reason not to learn anything new."

In other words, stay open-minded. Just relax and read. I'll make the learning process easy for you. In this book I will use hypnotic techniques to help you absorb this information at an accelerated rate. You may or may not notice these methods at work. If you're familiar with my earlier works, you may be onto my hidden methods. But know that this book is designed to speed up your learning so you can cut the 10-year training rule down to an almost instant improvement.

And now, when you're ready, let's go into our first trance.

THE WORLD'S LARGEST PRIVATE COLLECTION OF HYPNOSIS BOOKS

One day I checked my e-mail and found a brief note from someone called Stage Hypnotist Simone. I had never heard of him before. His e-mail was only two or three lines with a link. His message said, "Hi Joe. I'm selling my entire private collection of hypnosis books—about a half a ton worth—that I paid $30,000 to build. Go look at my eBay listing and tell your hypnotist friends to go look, too."

I instantly was curious. I went to the site, read over the brief description, and looked at the photo of the wall of books, magazines, and gadgets. The "buy it now" button on eBay was set for $8,000. I could bid a lower amount for the collection and I might win it, or I could click on the "buy it now" button and get it for $8,000. Even though there was no inventory listed for the collection, and the picture didn't give enough detail for me to even guess what I would be buying, I quickly e-mailed the seller and asked if we could talk.

He almost instantly replied back. Within seconds after that, we were on the phone.

"I'm a big fan of yours," he told me. "I have all of your books. I've followed your career online. I know you're a hybrid of marketing and hypnosis."

I immediately liked the guy.

"I know your coauthor, Bill Hibbler, too," he went on to say. Bill and I collaborated on the book *Meet and Grow Rich*. "I've talked to Bill in the past and admire his work, too."

We discussed the collection he was selling. He pointed out that much of the material was very old and no doubt now in the public domain. Some of the books sold on auction sites such as eBay sell for $300 a copy. He also had old magazines, signed books and letters from famed hypnotists, and much more.

We had a friendly conversation about hypnosis and magic that lasted only a few minutes before I decided to cut to the chase.

I probed to find out what he would accept for his collection. I still didn't know with any accuracy what was in the half ton of old books, but by now I was sold on them. I'm a collector, I'm a hypnotist, and this enormous collection would surely hold some gems for me. So I offered $5,000. Stage Hypnotist Simone—which is indeed his real name— asked for $6,000. I agreed.

Now stop and consider what happened here:

I got an e-mail from a complete stranger and less than 30 minutes later was agreeing to send him $6,000 for a collection of books I hadn't even seen an inventory of.

How did that happen?

The short answer is this: I went into a Buying Trance.

Let's examine how that happened:

1. I received an e-mail about hypnosis books. That got my attention (an important first step in creating a trance) because I'm obviously interested in the subject.

2. The actual e-mail was addressed to me personally, and not to "Dear Friend." Deepening rapport is a guaranteed way to induce a trance. A person's own name is very commanding and attention-getting.

3. The eBay listing, while skimpy on details, spoke to my key interests: books, magic, hypnosis, hypnotherapy. If you were to do a Google search of my brain, those would be the keywords to light up my neurons.

4. When we spoke on the phone, my trance state stayed deep because Stage Hypnotist Simone stroked my ego and again stayed focused on me and my desires.

5. He also mentioned such facts as some of the material being out of print and in the public domain, which would interest me because of my entrepreneurial activity of publishing old books and courses online.

In short, the entire experience, brief as it was, clearly demonstrated a Buying Trance at work.

Before you let yourself get too critical of this true story, consider instead how you can create this type of experience in the people you want to sell your products or service. It can be as easy as what happened with me and a complete stranger.

Let's find out how.

THE MAN WITH THE GOLDEN HELMET

I was watching an unusual documentary one night about belief. It was called *Mana: Beyond Belief*. It focused on people, places, cultures, and rituals from around the world. It showed followers of Elvis, believers in the Shroud of Turin, cherry blossom festivals in Japan, unnerving rituals in Africa, a man in India installing a new computer by blessing it, and much more. Pretty fascinating.

At one point the movie revealed the behind-the-scenes story of a famous painting, thought to be by Rembrandt, called *The Man with the Golden Helmet*. According to the film, the painting was so popular people would crowd the gallery room, three rows deep, straining to get just a peek at it. Advertisers used the image to sell products. The masterpiece became famous worldwide.

But then a group of researchers painstakingly analyzed the

painting. They finally concluded the work was not by Rembrandt at all, and could not have been.

Suddenly the crowds dwindled. No one cared about the man with the golden helmet. While the painting still hangs in a gallery in Germany, few pay any attention to it. It's still the same piece of art. Reproductions of it are still sold around the world.

But now the original doesn't draw a crowd.

Why?

THE BOOK

Years ago a friend of mine who produces a nationally syndicated television show walked into his boss's office and dropped a book on the desk. He wanted to make a point. But he didn't say a word. He just stood there.

"What's this?" his boss asked.

"A book."

"I can see that," his boss replied. "What about it?"

"Do you want to read it?"

"Not without knowing something about it," his boss replied.

"Yeah, that's the point," my friend said, and he walked out.

What did he mean?

What was his point?

BLOTNICK'S LIE

In one of my latest books, *The Attractor Factor*, I recount the story of Srully Blotnick, an author and researcher of many best-selling books. Dr. Blotnick often wrote about a study done proving that people who follow their dreams make more money than those who pursue money. It's a fascinating report. It's inspiring. It's one of the favorite sections in my own book.

But the story, I'm told now, is a myth.

Apparently Blotnick never did the research.

According to Susan Faludi, author of *Backlash: The Undeclared War Against American Women*, although Blotnick wrote several respected books and they were all published by reputable publishers, and he even wrote a column for *Forbes* magazine for 10 years, he was later found to be a fraud.

Those who read about his work today but who don't know the punch line are inspired to pursue their dreams, just like the people in his supposed study.

But those who read his work today and know of his later debunking don't feel so inspired.

Why is that?

Before I start to unravel this apparent contradiction of mesmerizing stories, let me share one more with you.

BIG FAT LIARS

In a book I read a while back called *Big Fat Liars*, author Morris Chafetz recounts the story of a book that awakened everyone to the true story behind the supposed gun culture in the United States. The book, *Arming America*, claimed to use probate records to prove that prior to 1850 fewer than 10 percent of Americans owned guns, and fully half of those guns didn't work.

The book was a major hit. Scholars praised the book. Columbia University gave the author the prestigious Bancroft Prize for History. Chicago's Newberry Library awarded the author a $30,000 fellowship. The applause continued until one day someone questioned the author's research.

According to *Big Fat Liars*, the author of *Arming America* had fabricated his research. When confronted, he said his notes from probate records had been destroyed in a flood. He couldn't prove his claims. When backed into a corner by investigators, he kept changing his story. Ultimately, his Bancroft Prize was withdrawn. His book died, too.

What happened?

What's the theme within all of the preceding stories, anyway?

Before you leap ahead, stop and describe what you think is going on in these stories:

_____

_____

_____

_____

_____

THE ULTIMATE SECRET

Brace yourself. What I'm about to tell you may be the greatest marketing lesson of all time.

It ties into my often-stated belief that "Most of marketing is perception."

Yes, you need a good product.

Yes, you need to fulfill your promises to people.

But what will influence people more than anything else—in their purchasing and in their satisfaction—is their *perception*.

Consider the following:

- Rembrandt's painting was perceived to be great while it was perceived to be by Rembrandt. As soon as it was discovered to be a fake, interest dropped. It was no longer perceived as valuable, even though it's a masterful painting and still hangs in an art gallery.

- My friend could not get his boss to read the book he brought him because there was no framing for the book. It was simply "a book," something unknown, so there was no perception of any real value.

- The gun control book was perceived as a breakthrough as long as people perceived the research was truthful. As soon as it was revealed to be a hoax, the book and author lost all respect, and sales dropped.

- Blotnick's work was respected and popularized by many, including me, until it was discovered that he may have fabricated his studies. As a result, perception of him went from holy to humbug.

Are you beginning to grasp the secret?

Are you beginning to see a pattern here?

Perceptions control how people respond to anything, and their perceptions are largely controlled by others.

Who controls their perceptions?

Need I answer that?

Well, maybe I do.

So let's continue.

When you walk into a grocery store and choose one brand of toothpaste over another, the pretty packaging is only part of what activates your decision to buy. The rest was programmed into your mind over time through advertising and publicity, the strong arms of marketing that you rarely paid conscious attention to, causing you to create a perception. That perception created the urge to buy (or not).

Who's in control here?

Who's pulling the strings to make us buy?

Who's the wizard behind the curtain, anyway?

Could it be—*you*?

A NEW PSYCHOLOGY

What I'm suggesting is that people are—let's be blunt—machines.

They are not awake.

Yes, their eyes are open.

Yes, they can think.

But the vast majority of their actions are stemming from unconscious motivations. Even *they* don't know why they do what they do. Ask them and they'll give you a reason, but it's rarely the accurate one.

Hypnotists know this. Put someone into a trance and plant the suggestion to open a window when the phone rings. Tell them to forget that the suggestion was installed but to act on it. When the phone rings, they'll do as you suggested. Ask them why they did it, and they'll rationalize their behavior, saying something such as, "I suddenly felt warm."

The real reason they acted will be hidden from even them!

I don't mean this to sound negative. I mean it to be realistic.

Clotaire Rapaille gives another example in his book, *The Culture Code*. He says the nineteenth-century scientist Jean-Martin Charcot hypnotized a person, handed her an umbrella, and asked her to open it. He then awakened her. She was surprised to see the object in her hand. Charcot asked why she had an open umbrella indoors. The woman was baffled. But all she could think to say was, "It was raining." The woman was not stupid. She simply had to justify what she did in *some* way.

Rapaille writes, "Even the most self-examining of us are rarely in close contact with our subconscious. We have little interaction with this powerful force that drives so many of our actions. Therefore, we give answers to questions that sound logical and are even what the questioner expected, but which don't reveal the unconscious forces that preconditioned our feelings."

The branch of psychology that deals with cognitive behavior states that people act because of their thinking processes, which of course involves their perceptions. My argument is that someone *other* than the person thinking is creating most of those perceptions. In a real way, marketing is the hypnotist and the consumers are the subjects.

This is why we need to understand public relations, marketing, and advertising. These fields are used not just to influence perception, but to actually create it.

This chapter is simply an introduction to the concept of mind control through intentional marketing. This is all about putting people into what I call a Buying Trance. That's what you'll learn about in this book, the first ever written on this new psychology of sales and marketing.

Before I end this chapter and dive into the meat of this book, let me be sure you understand what I'm saying here.

Let's cut to the chase:

THE BOTTOM LINE

Here's a working theory to get started:

How you frame, position, or explain your product or service will determine how people perceive it. How they perceive it will determine what they do.

Let me repeat that:

How you frame, position, or explain your product or service will determine how people perceive it. How they perceive it will determine what they do.

Your marketing creates a type of Buying Trance that people fall into (as long as they trust you) and will stay in until something shakes them awake.

Please don't think this is obvious. I've been involved in marketing almost 30 years. I've taken part in everything from infomercials to radio spots to direct mail campaigns to Internet breakthroughs. I'm considered the father of hypnotic writing and hypnotic marketing, and wrote books on both subjects. I've taught thousands of people how to get results through their marketing. I've written more books than I care to list. I've recorded audio programs, taught seminars, held events, and even have my own Executive Mentoring Program and Hypnotic Gold, my own membership program. I've spent half a lifetime learning, teaching, and practicing marketing.

Yet I'm constantly surprised when people overlook such basic and obvious things as having a business card or putting their contact information on a sales letter. Just the other day someone sent me an 11-page letter and ended it by asking me to call them.

But they left off their phone number!

So don't think *any* of this is obvious.

Instead, look for ways to use these insights today to build your own empire.

After all, aren't *you* awake while everyone else is asleep?

POSITIVE EXPECTANCY

Let me give you one final example.

When I was ready to turn in one of my earlier books, *Life's Missing Instruction Manual: The Guidebook You Should Have Been Given at Birth*, to my publisher, I wanted to put the editors into a Buying Trance.

Most publishers are typically conservative and short-sighted. They can't guess what the public will want and are fearful about taking risks. Rather than turning in a cold manuscript—much like my friend and the book he dropped on his boss's desk—I decided to turn in a manuscript with a dozen endorsements in front of it. So I wrote to some people, asked them to look at the manuscript, and collected their testimonials.

Why?

Obviously, those early positive reviews will put the editors into a type of *positive expectancy*—a trance where they are more likely to look at the pile of pages I hand them as maybe being actually good. Yes, the book was and is good. But I wanted the *perception* that the book is good to be there *first*. Following that, the book may even be considered *great*.

I did something similar with this very work you're reading.

Can you guess what it was?

Write your answer here:

_____

_____

_____

_____

What did I do to influence your perception about this chapter?

Look back to the opening pages of this book. You'll see testimonials. That is designed to set the stage for your perception. It's there to lead your mind in the direction I want it to go: to begin thinking of this book as being a breakthrough in powerful marketing.

Do you see how this works?

What I've shared with you here may be the greatest sales and marketing secret of all time. It goes beyond current expectations of sales and right into the psychology of mythmaking.

Unless you create a story, a framing, a positioning, you will not gain entrance to, let alone a lasting place in, the mind of your consumer.

I shouldn't have to add that your positioning must be honest. If you fabricate stories or data to get attention, sooner or later someone will blow the whistle on you. When they do, you'll feel the sting. And it may last a long, long time.

Instead, come from your heart, appeal to the emotions, and always stay true.

And now let me challenge you with something important.

YOUR CHALLENGE

Here's something else to chew on and to keep you up tonight wondering about:

I've used this chapter to establish at least one perception within you.

Whether you agree with that bold assertion or not, assume I know what I'm doing and that I installed a perception in you through these very words.

What is it?

Or is there more than one?

Write your answer here, or on a sheet of paper someplace near you:

_____

_____

_____

_____

Give up?

Let me give you a clue:

Think back to what you read here so far and consider what you now want to know more about.

Write down your thoughts, ideas, and insights:

_____

_____

_____

_____

Now here's the million-dollar question:

Did what I wrote in this chapter create that interest?

In other words, did this writing create that perception in you?

Maybe consider the question this way:

Did you have that interest *before* reading this chapter?

I'll let you wonder about the answer to that. But note what you do over the next hour or so after reading this chapter.

Finally, my purpose here has been to introduce you to one of the most powerful and maybe even darkest marketing secrets of all time. I trust you will use it to brighten the world. After all, people are waiting to be led. (They're machines, remember.) Lead them to greatness, and lead yourself to riches.

Carry the torch to victory.

Remember . . .

Bene agendo nuquam defessus.

(Never weary of doing good.)

THE TRUTH ABOUT WHY PEOPLE BUY

B efore you learn about the Buying Trance, it would help to have a foundation about the nature of human psychology as most people currently understand it. Based on my own experience in business, I'd say Abraham Maslow is the reigning king in business psychology. The troubling fact, though, is he's wrong.

MASLOW WAS WRONG

Abraham Maslow is best known for his famous hierarchy of needs. One of the many interesting things Maslow noticed while he worked with monkeys early in his career was that some needs take top billing over others. For example, if you are hungry and thirsty, you will usually take care of the thirst first. After all, you can do without food for weeks, but you can do without water for maybe a couple of days. Thirst is a stronger need than hunger, according to Maslow.

By the same token, if you are thirsty, but someone is choking you and you can't breathe, which is more important—water or air? Obviously, the need to breathe. Immediate survival is more important than quenching your thirst. Sex is less powerful than any of these, at least in Maslow's opinion. In short, you don't need it as much. To help you understand his model, here's Maslow's famous chart.

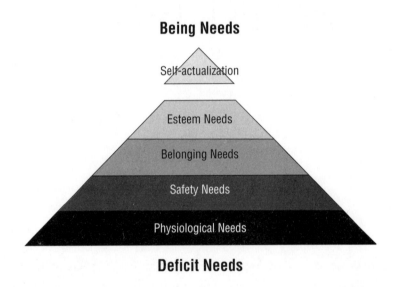

Being Needs

Self-actualization

Esteem Needs

Belonging Needs

Safety Needs

Physiological Needs

Deficit Needs

If you don't think about it too much, Maslow's chart looks logical. But let's take a closer look.

Robert Fritz, the author of *Creating* and *The Path of Least Resistance*, once told me that Maslow was wrong. Fritz said, "Look at rap music. It's a new form of creativity and it came from the ghetto, where kids still experience hunger, thirst, and poverty. They didn't need to actualize first. They need to express first."

Fritz isn't the only person to disagree with Maslow. Steven Reiss, in his book, *Who Am I?*, discusses 16 basic desires that motivate people. They don't match Maslow's model. The basic desires Reiss found are:

Power	Social contact
Independence	Family
Curiosity	Status
Acceptance	Vengeance
Order	Romance
Saving	Eating
Honor	Physical Exercise
Idealism	Tranquility

Interestingly enough, William James, the great American psychologist, listed the following desires in his epic work of 1890, *The Principles of Psychology*:

Saving	Play
Construction	Sex
Curiosity	Shame
Exhibition	Pain Avoidance
Family	Herd
Hunting	Vengeance
Order	

Obviously, not all concerns are equal in the eye of each beholder. You and your customers and clients will focus on some desires over others. They won't all compel you to take action. You may be more interested in exercise than in eating, or, as in my case, the reverse.

You'll need to know what your prospects are most interested in to be able to create a Buying Trance that captivates them. That's where research comes into the picture. For now, understanding what really motivates people is the foundation to understanding this new psychology of marketing and selling. While Maslow offered a hierarchical model that doesn't seem accurate, James and Reiss offer lists of core desires that seem to have stood the test of time. But I don't want to stop there. Let's look at this area a little more deeply now.

THE TOP FIVE REASONS

Elmer Wheeler, famed "sell the sizzle, not the steak" salesman and author, described five psychological motivators in 1948 in his book, *Tested Salesmanship*. These five hot buttons are still trance inducers today. They are:

1. *Importance.* Wheeler used psychologist Alfred Adler as evidence that the number one motivator for people is the search to feel superior.

2. *Appreciation.* People leave their jobs and their spouses to find this hot button elsewhere.

3. *Approval.* Wheeler explained that we all want to be liked by other people. Most people will torture themselves (such as going on a strict diet) to attain this sense of approval from others.

4. *Ease.* People are lazy. As a result, they want things easily, quickly, and even instantaneously. Wheeler suggested that the quest for ease might be the story of evolution itself.

5. *Success.* People want whatever "success" means to them. It could be money, security, a bigger house, a better insurance plan, or many other things.

Wheeler understood people better than most psychologists of his time. He knew that if you did your selling and marketing with one of the five motivators in mind, the chances of a sell were high.

WHO NEEDS A BATHTUB?

To put this in perspective, in 1880 few American homes had a bathtub or even running water. A few manufacturers began to advertise bathtubs, but people did not want them. Some states even placed a tax on them. One state passed a law making it illegal to have a bathtub. Over time, persistent advertising changed people's minds. Today it's rare for an American home not to have a bathtub.

The point is this: When you attempt to market anything to anyone, unless you address them *at their current trance level*, you will not be accepted by them. Those early advertisers of bathtubs were speaking to people in a trance ("bathtubs are bad") and not connecting to that trance. Repetition—which is a hypnotic technique—can get the message through, but only over time and at great expense. A better way is to remember that people are in a trance, and to use one of their core desires to reach them and awaken them.

Let's explore this even more deeply.

THE 26 REASONS PEOPLE BUY

Why do people buy anything?

What are they hoping to achieve when they spend their money?

The following list is from my book, *The AMA Complete Guide to Small Business Advertising*. If you appeal to one or more of the following 26 reasons people buy anything, you will get more of their money. Why? Because you will *automatically* begin to lead them into a Buying Trance. You will be speaking to their current trance, or interests.

1. To make money.
2. To save money.
3. To save time.
4. To avoid effort.
5. To get more comfort.
6. To achieve greater cleanliness.
7. To attain better health.
8. To escape physical pain.

9. To gain praise.

10. To be popular.

11. To attract the opposite sex.

12. To conserve possessions.

13. To increase enjoyment.

14. To gratify curiosity.

15. To protect family.

16. To be in style.

17. To have or hold beautiful possessions.

18. To satisfy appetite.

19. To emulate others.

20. To avoid trouble.

21. To avoid criticism.

22. To be individual.

23. To protect reputation.

24. To take advantage of opportunities.

25. To have safety.

26. To make work easier.

Of course, just having this list doesn't help you create or complete a Buying Trance. What it does is help you *begin* one.

Before you learn how to create a Buying Trance, review the list of reasons. See if what you are currently selling ties in to one or more of the 26 reasons people buy anything. Being aware of their motivation and the connection to your business is a key first step in understanding the Buying Trance.

But it's only the *first* step.

Keep reading to learn more.

THE NUDE
WIZARD OF
MONEYMAKING
APPEAL

R oy Garn was a genius. You may never have heard of him until now. Yet he's been one of the most influential thinkers in my business when it comes to the psychology of the Buying Trance. It was Roy Garn who taught me that everyone—even you—is preoccupied. The genius of Garn was that he spelled out exactly what you are preoccupied with. He said there were four things that could be on your mind at any one time.

Can you guess what they are?

Before I explain them to you, let me tell you a little about Garn and his work.

THE MAGIC OF ROY GARN

Roy Garn wrote the book *The Magic Power of Emotional Appeal* in 1960. It went through 10 printings by 1964. It was released in hardcover and paperback, and became a book club selection. Today the book is largely forgotten.

I have read the book five or six times. While some people in business read Napoleon Hill's classic work, *Think and Grow Rich*, multiple times, my own personal favorite for repeat readings is Roy Garn's *The Magic Power of Emotional Appeal*. To me, it is a life-changing classic.

I've never been able to learn anything about Garn. I've done the obvious Google searches on him. I've even hired a private investigator to locate Garn or any of his relatives. He didn't find a thing. I also hired Google researchers to locate Garn. They couldn't find anything, either. I've done library searches, written publishers and other authors, and more. Nothing. Garn has disappeared. I've often wondered, jokingly, if Garn went into some sort of witness protection program. He's gone.

Fortunately, though, his masterpiece remains, at least in used book stores and sometimes on eBay. If you can get a copy of his book, do so. It will help teach you about the core essence of the Buying Trance. As Roy Garn wrote in his book:

"Remember that Preoccupation is the bugaboo of your existence and that everybody is preoccupied!"

SELLING TO EMOTIONS

What I love about Garn's message is the simplicity of it, coupled with his memorable illustrations. Let me give you a few examples:

Garn talks about four lingerie shops on the same block in the same city, all selling the same type of nightgowns. This was intense competition.

What would *you* do to sell more gowns than your competition?

One store hung signs on two racks. One sign said, "For Sinners!" The other sign said, "For Saints."

In three days the store sold out of all of the nightgowns.

Two newspaper stands stood beside each other, competing for customers. One seller said "Next" after every sale. The other said "Thank you" after every sale.

The latter sold four times as many newspapers.

At a meeting of businesspeople, an otherwise normal-looking gent was introduced as "A *killer* from Brooklyn!"

The audience was riveted. They wanted to know who the killer was.

The man turned out to be an exterminator.

In one area of the country, people kept speeding, even when the signs on the road clearly said the speed limit was 20 miles per hour. Finally someone suggested a new sign. It read: "20 mph or $19.95 fine!"

Everyone slowed down.

An owner of a parking garage in a big city couldn't get people to park in his lot. He tried putting up signs saying, "Parking" and "Park Here." But few people parked there.

What would you have done?

The owner put up a new sign, this one with some emotional appeal in it. It read: "PROTECTED Parking."

Sales increased at once.

In each of these examples, emotional appeal is being used to take people from their state of mental preoccupation into a new state: a Buying Trance.

This is the genius of Roy Garn.

THE FATAL FOUR

What are people preoccupied with?

Garn revealed the "fatal four" (as he called them) preoccupations of each of us in his book. He said they are:

1. Self-preservation

2. Romance

3. Money

4. Recognition

According to Garn, all buying decisions and motivators fall into one or more of those four categories. That's it. If that's true, and I certainly believe it is, then knowing them can help you quickly get someone into a Buying Trance. With that in mind, let's look at each preoccupation.

SELF-PRESERVATION

Self-preservation is health, security, protection of yourself/ belongings/family, and anything else dealing with your ability to keep what's yours and live forever. This is the hot button that sells everything from insurance to security systems to fitness products and more. Garn wrote: "It includes fears, hopes, and wishes within attitudes about personal satisfactions, comforts, danger, pain, sickness, health, death, or injury."

He added that self-preservation "includes love of parent for child, child for parent, master for pet, and related protective feelings. Desires for personal freedom and fears of imprisonment are in this appeal; so are most aspects of religious belief and communication."

ROMANCE

Romance, as you might easily imagine, involves sex. But Garn was clear when he pointed out that sex itself falls under the category of self-preservation while sexual desire and attraction fall under romance.

Garn explained that this one "fatal flaw" could overrule all others when done right. In his book he cited the following example about a newspaper:

> A four-column story screams: "PRESIDENT SUBMITS NEW BUDGET." A two-column story reads: "TWO PARADES ON SUNDAY." One column is headed: "FIGHTER FIGHTS FOR LIFE." Half-column is topped by: "STRIKE TALKS ON." A smaller two-inch story carries the headline: "NUDE REDHEAD FOUND ALIVE."

Garn then asks, "Which story will most readers read *first* and remember *best*?"

Obviously, sex gets attention. It breaks the preoccupation people are in because it ties into their preexisting desires: either to feel the attraction of sex (romance) or to feel the completion of sex (self-preservation.)

But romance didn't end there for Garn. He said this emotional appeal also involved "the Future Promise" and "the Desire for New Experiences." Garn wrote:

> Whether in love, health, money, appearance, satisfaction, or recognition, we all strive towards some form of perfection. Those whose words and actions help us move mentally in the direction of our personal preferences offer us more of the happiness we seek.

Garn explained that when you paint a picture of a future people want to experience, you are tapping into romance. The same is true when you offer a new experience that people feel a desire to have. You are, in essence, romancing them.

MONEY

Money should not surprise you as a motivator. It's not the only one, and it's not always the most powerful one, but it certainly goes on the list as one of the top four movers and shakers in the field of persuasion.

Garn tells the following story to illustrate the power of the money appeal:

> An organization was formed in Stuttgart, called the *League of the Long*. It consisted of men 6'2" and over, and women 5'11" and taller. Members estimated that it cost 15% more to feed a big man and 10% more for a big woman, as compared to people of average stature and appetite. The *League* appealed to the government for tax reduction because they ate more than other people!

Anything having to do with making or saving money gets attention. If tied in with romance, self-preservation, or recognition, it becomes all the more powerful and even irresistible. Garn wrote:

> The deep wish, want and desire is to have Money. The fear, hate or uncertainty is to be without Money or to part with it unexpectedly. We are most emotionally receptive to the person who suggests ways for us to get more.

RECOGNITION

But money isn't the only motivator, and may not be the most powerful one. Very often people will do things simply to be noticed. This is the power of recognition.

Garn wrote:

> In human communication, the Emotional Appeal of Recognition can instantly break Preoccupation, enter a mind or change a mind. It relates to pride, opinion, appreciation, identification with clothing, appearance, behavior, events, people, products or organizations. It embraces emotional tie-ins to loneliness, popularity and the way you appear "in the eyes of others." Looking "good" to others is important to *us*.

Recognizing someone can put them into the early stages of a Buying Trance. Garn suggested that listening to someone with your eyes and ears makes them feel important or recognized. He wrote, "If you sincerely want to be better-liked by them, show that you ARE impressed by their words, actions or possessions."

Here's an example of the power of recognition. In every situation there is an unseen and unconscious play of status. One person is perceived as higher and the other is perceived as lower. This happens virtually all the time. When you start to become aware of it, you'll see it everywhere. You can also use this to your advantage. When you intentionally lower your status, others will feel comfortable around you. They will like you and want to spend more time with you. They feel safe. They feel important. They feel respected. They feel recognized.

In early 2006 I got to meet superstar actor James Caan. I love Caan as an actor. He's been in such classic movies as *Rollerball* and of course *The Godfather*. But I really admired him as a person when we were in his trailer on the studio lot of the *Las Vegas* TV show, and he asked my opinion about a new reality-TV show he's currently involved in. He asked . . . and he listened.

On top of that, he did some brainstorming with me, showing that my opinion counted. I disagreed with him about something he was doing to market the reality show, and he didn't argue. He heard me out. He told me his view. I told him mine. We had a discussion. When you consider that I'm a nobody in his world and he's a deity in the movie and television world, the fact that we had *any* discussion is amazing.

In short, Caan lowered his status to let little ole me feel more at home in his neon-lit world. This was a major feat, and something I will never forget. He *recognized* me.

I have no idea if James Caan did this intentionally or not. I like to think he really wanted my opinion. It doesn't matter. It made for one of those experiences you write home about. It was an example of the power of recognition. Garn would have loved it. He wrote: "No matter who you are, belittle yourself—not your listener. Admit that you're *not* very smart and most people will like you, because you confess *their* superiority."

As you can obviously conclude, knowing these "fatal four" preoccupation windows into a person's mind is a guaranteed way to begin a Buying Trance. But to more completely understand how this psychology works, it's time to wander into the world of the Buying Trance itself.

How I
Discovered the
Buying Trance

I couldn't snap Billy out of his trance.

It happened more than 30 years ago. I was a teenager fascinated by the powers of the mind. I read about spirituality, psychic phenomena, unidentified flying objects (UFOs), past lives, present problems, the magic of believing, and, yes, even hypnosis.

And that helps explain why I had my best friend, Billy, in a deep trance in the basement of my parents' home in Ohio. I had regressed him from the age of 16 back to the age of 4 or 5. I had no business doing it. But I was curious and Billy was game. It was a remarkable morning until something truly terrifying happened.

I snapped my fingers—the prearranged command to wake Billy up—but he stayed in the chair, smiling, eyes closed, and laughing loud and hard.

"How old are you?" I asked, wanting to check his age level.

"Seventy-two, how old are you?!" he replied, laughing like a wild, untamed, truly obnoxious child.

You can't imagine my fear.

"When I slap my hands together, you will awaken," I commanded.

Billy laughed long and loud.

I slapped my hands together.

Billy laughed louder and longer.

I was panicking now. I was barely sixteen years old. I had my best friend in a hypnotic trance, regressed to a young age, and I couldn't bring him out of it. I could see my parents' rage. I could see Billy's parents' rage. I could see myself locked up, still a teenager, all because I had practiced hypnosis while other kids played baseball or Monopoly.

I waited. I held my breath. I snapped my fingers. I slapped my hands. I perspired. Billy wasn't coming out of his trance. He was locked into another time period. And I was responsible.

Some kids borrow the neighbor's car and wreck it. I borrowed my best friend's mind and put it in park.

What was I going to do?

I don't recall how much time went by before I decided to call for help. I remember going to the phone book and desperately searching for a hypnotist to call. I found one in Cleveland, Ohio, a hundred miles from my home. I called him, got him on the phone, and acted as cool as I could.

"Doctor, my name is Joe, and, well, I've been learning about hypnosis," I began. "I was just wondering, what would happen if you put someone in a trance and they, well, er, ah, you know, never came out of it?"

There was silence on the line.

Then I remember the voice bellowing at me.

"Are you practicing hypnosis there?!"

"Oh, no," I lied. "I was just curious what would happen if, you know, you put your best friend under, regressed him, and he wouldn't come out of it. Is that a bad thing?"

"Is your best friend there now?"

The hypnotist was onto me.

"Well . . . yes."

"Will he come to the phone?"

"He won't do *anything* I ask," I said. My voice was cracking now. I was scared and it showed.

"Don't worry about it," the hypnotist advised me. "He'll either naturally awaken shortly, or he'll fall asleep and then wake up."

"But he thinks he's five years old," I added.

"You kids have to stop playing around!" he roared.

"But I want to be a hypnotist someday," I explained.

"Get training first!" he snapped.

"Okay, okay, I will," I said. "But what do I do about Billy?"

"Put him on the phone."

I went to Billy and somehow got him to get on the phone, and the hypnotist said something that helped Billy awaken. To this day I don't know what he said. And since I haven't seen Billy in nearly 20 years, I have no idea how old Billy really thinks he is. I understand he's now a state trooper in Ohio, so I imagine he's stable and well. Still, I'm staying in Texas.

I learned something profound that day in my parents' basement when my life stopped for a morning.

I learned that hypnotic trances are powerful. They are real. And we are all in them.

That's right. You're in a trance. Yes, right now. So am I. We may not think we're five years old, but we think we are writers, or marketers, or salespeople, or some other "trance." As long as we believe the trance we are in, we will play it out perfectly. When we wake up, we'll just be in another trance. Even the "I'm now awake" trance is just another trance.

Stay with me here. Whether you disagree or not, there's a valuable lesson here—one that can help you increase your sales and your profits.

In short, your prospects are all in trances. If you merge with their trance, you can then lead them out of it and into the Buying Trance you want them to be in.

I'll repeat that:

"Your prospects are all in trances. If you merge with their trance, you can then lead them out of it and into the Buying Trance you want them to be in."

Let me explain with an example:

Say you want to sell a new software program on how to incorporate a business. How would you do it? The average person might send out a sales letter that says, "New program makes incorporating a snap." That approach would get some sales, especially from people already wanting to incorporate.

But a more hypnotic approach would be to run a headline such as this: "Tired of paying too much in taxes? Read this surprising way out of the maze!" This new approach would merge with the existing trance in a businessperson.

In other words, they are in the "taxes suck" trance and the "small businesses get screwed" trance. Agree with them. Merge with them. Accept that trance as your door. Then lead into what you want to sell by tying it back to their trance.

Let's break down this process into three steps:

1. What do your prospects believe right now? (Current trance.)

2. Agree with their beliefs to merge with them. (Rapport.)

3. Lead their beliefs into your offer. (New trance.)

That's it. That's the real secret to hypnotic selling using the Buying Trance.

What? Oh. You want another example? Here goes:

Say you want to sell a pair of pants. How would you use our Buying Trance three-step process to move them?

Step 1: What do your prospect's believe right now about pants?

A little research would help. Let's say they believe all pants are the same. They are in the "all pants are alike" trance. That's their current trance, or mind-set. You would not be very wise to argue with it. Instead, accept it and go to step 2.

Step 2: Agree with them.

In person, on the phone, or in your headlines, say something that lets your prospects know you are in the same trance. Use statements such as, "I thought all pants were alike, too" or "No pants are different—so why even look at this pair?" This creates rapport. You can't sell anyone without creating rapport. So, step 2 is a way to meet people where they are. Consciously join their unconscious trance. Then go to the next step.

Step 3: Now lead them into your offer.

You might say something like, "Why are people saying these pants are different? Here's why." This is taking them into a new trance—a trance that says, "Some pants are different"—a Buying Trance. Because you have acknowledged the trance they were in and merged with them, you are now in a position—a very powerful position—to sell them.

There are numerous ways to find people's trances, merge with them, and then lead them into a "buy from you" trance. I won't be able to go into all of them in this short chapter. I'm just giving you the tip of the iceberg here. But before I end, let's look at possible existing trances your prospects may be in when you call or send them a sales piece. They include:

"I'm worried about money" trance.

"I'm lonely" trance.

"I'm afraid of people" trance.

"I'm sick and tired of my job" trance.

"I'm fed up with my kids" trance.

"The world sucks" trance.

"I'm hungry" trance.

"I need to lose weight" trance.

And so it goes. You'll notice that each of these trances is self-serving. That's the nature of people. They are interested in their well-being first. They are preoccupied with their own needs, desires, pains, and more.

Any inward state is a trance. Naturally, everyone is in one trance or another when you call them or write them. Your job is to note it, merge with it, and lead them out of it.

Here's one final example to make this process clearer for you.

Let's say you want to sell a music recording. We'll make it a classical CD.

Step 1: What trance are people already in?

You can imagine they come home from work, find your sales letter in their mail, and are *not* in the mood for it. Your headline might say, "Just got home from work?"

Step 2: Create rapport by acknowledging their trance.

You might write, "Since you just got home from work, you are probably tired and ready to toss this mail in the trash. But wait one second before you do it."

Step 3: Now introduce your new trance.

Maybe write: "Imagine putting a CD on that fills your mind with soothing, relaxing, healing music, the kind of heavenly sounds that help you drift far, far away from your day. . . ."

To end this chapter, let me remind you of what Billy taught me when I was a kid:

Everyone is in a trance and everyone can be brought out of it. The idea is not to ignore this quirk of human nature, but to use it for the well-being of all you touch—including your own profit. What you can do is take people from their existing trances into your Buying Trance. The rest of this book will show you exactly how to do that.

Just don't age regress any of your prospects!

How to Uncover Someone's Current Trance

You should be wondering at this point how to de-termine the current trance someone is in. After all, if the preceding chapter proved that you create a Buying Trance by first merging with an existing trance, how do you uncover someone's existing trance?

Good question. To help arrive at an answer you can take to the bank, I went to some experts in the field of selling, marketing, persuasion, and hypnosis. Here are their answers.

Craig Perrine, of www.maverickmarketer.com, a well-known Internet marketer, said:

Not only are people in a preoccupied state, but they are telling themselves stories about what is going on in their lives. For example, this happened to me the other day.

I was hopelessly stuck trying to dream up a headline for a very important product launch. I stared at my laptop screen until my eyes throbbed and my hands fell asleep.

The phone was ringing constantly and several client-related projects were also weighing on my mind, so I continued to draw a blank.

Out of desperation I took the phone off the hook, and then I remembered a secret weapon I had in my arsenal—a special CD developed by an audio genius friend of mine that synchronizes the brainwaves for maximum creativity and focus.

I popped on my headphones, and presto, within minutes my mind was like a laser-guided copywriting machine coming up with one great line after another.

Sure enough, I wrote a headline that worked like gangbusters . . . and it was effortless.

And in that story I just told you I used my favorite "trance matching" technique. See, you're reading this book because you are interested in marketing. Knowing that, I bet you are also frustrated at times with the challenge of coming up with winning promotions. Knowing that, I told you a story you about a problem I bet you related to.

As a marketer, my goal was to tell you about the CD product, but if I had started talking about the CD before I had drawn you in to my trance, the odds are much higher that you'd ignore my message. So, if you just read that story and identified with my writer's block predicament and wanted to get your hands on that audio CD I used to bang out the winning headline, then you just entered the trance I intended.

I did that so you could experience my favorite technique firsthand. Telling a personal story about overcoming a problem you and your target customer share is a powerful technique for drawing someone into your desired trance and leading them to a buying decision.

The more your story sounds like their story, the more they'll feel you have something in common, and the more they'll stop what they are doing, pay attention to what you have to say, and buy from you.

Note: The audio CD Craig mentions is called *Audio Espresso: Getting It Done Now*. It's by Pat O'Bryan. See www.milagroresearchinstitute.com/AE.htm.

Daniel Levis, a copywriter at www.sellingtohumanna-ture.com, replied:

My favorites are forums. I wrote a sales letter for an investment newsletter recently. It's called Gold Newsletter, and it's targeted at a very small subculture. To research what this niche was thinking I visited this discussion board: http://forum.whiskeyandgunpowder .com/viewforum.php?f=1&sid=91bdafb47eebe05acfd64d20c45a22e2.

David Garfinkel, of www.world-copywriting-institute.com, a famous copywriter and online marketer, said:

I look for signals in two areas: what prospects or customers really want and how ready they are to buy.

It's the rare customer who can tell you straight-out what they really want. Usually if you ask people directly what they are look-ing for, they will have a cover story, something that masks their true desires. Most of the time this isn't on purpose, at least at a conscious level.

Over the years, people have learned to protect themselves from getting taken advantage of by unscrupulous sellers, by sending out verbal decoys instead of fully expressing what they want immediately after being asked.

I find it's a long question-and-answer process to get to the heart of the matter this way. Sometimes that's worth it, but often it's impractical.

What I have learned to do instead is rely on indirect signals that help me zero in on the true desires:

- *Stories people tell.* *If I ask someone to tell me a story about their situation or their experiences in the past, they will often reveal what they want and what they're willing to buy. People disclose a lot of valuable information in their stories that they hold back in straight answers.*

- *Complaints they make.* *People rarely censor themselves when they air their complaints. As they tell me what they don't like, it becomes a quick process of elimination to determine what they do want.*

- *Questions they ask.* *It's a mistake to think of questions solely as requests for information. They're also expressions of want and need, although the specific wants and needs are sometimes disguised.*

As for readiness to buy, certain specific questions—about delivery or starting date, payment terms, and specific features or terms and conditions—tell me a person is close to yes. Nonverbal signals in the voice, like the rate of speech, the tone of voice, and the energy level and confidence as a person speaks, are also reliable indicators of readiness to buy.

———

Mark Joyner, Internet legend and author of *The Great Formula* and *The Irresistible Offer*, said:

In print, you have to guess what kind of trance the reader is in. But, instead of guessing, you target those who you know are already in that trance.

One maxim I created years ago in the early days of Web market- ing was "All clicks are not created equal."

This simply means that each clicker is in a different kind of trance.

So, all you have to do is call out to those who are in the trance that is most conducive to a sale of your product.

You do this by targeting your advertising. In a multistep mar- keting process, you call out to those in the proper trance in your first step.

In your primary sales vehicle, you use a headline that calls out to people who are in the right trance.

The headline will alienate some people who aren't in that trance, but that's okay. They're unlikely to buy.

In person, you can ask people innocuous questions that are likely to reveal bias.

Questions about controversial topics asked in a neutral way but with emotion are great.

Here's an example.

"Man, what do you think about that stuff happening in the Mid- dle East?"

The way they answer not only will reveal their bias on the topic (notice that you didn't reveal yours), but will also say a lot about their disposition.

David Deutsch, of www.thinkinginside.com, well-known direct-response copywriter, said:

As a copywriter, I have to start, as Robert Collier says, with the con- versation already going on in the prospect's head.

How do I find out what that conversation is?

It's a three-step process.

First, I read everything I can that would help me find out. I read the magazines and books that they read. I read research and any- thing else that could give me insight into what they're thinking and feeling. I read other successful promotions to the same audience, which, because they were successful, help me infer how to tap into their thoughts and feelings.

Second, I try to talk to the prospects themselves. Maybe they are actual customers or prospects. Or maybe they are friends, relatives, or acquaintances I think fit the same profile. I engage them in a conversation about the product in a way that brings out how they think and feel about it and anything surrounding it. I try to sell them on the product so I can see what thoughts and emotions it brings up.

The third and final step is to try to become the prospect. I sit quietly and imagine I possess the characteristics and circumstances of my target audience. And I see what I think and how I feel about the category the product falls into (health or investing, for example); items in the news related to the category (new health discoveries or the recent market downturn, for example); the product itself; the problem the product solves; the benefits the product brings; and so on.

Pat O'Bryan of www.patobryan.com said:

I cheat.

I listen.

Most people will let you know right away what state they're in by the words they choose to describe what they're experiencing. Do things "look" good? Does that "sound" great? Maybe it "feels" funny.

Further clues are in the pacing and speed of speech. My working theory is that the states have speeds—visual is fastest, kinesthetic is slowest. If somebody is speaking really slowly, they're probably in a kinesthetic state.

And, of course, there are the eyes. I used to carry around an eye chart from a Richard Bandler book and sneak peeks at it while I was talking to people. It's uncanny how much you can tell from people's eye movements—even when you tell them what you're doing.

When I'm writing, it depends on what I'm writing.

If I'm writing a sales page, I've got a chance in the preliminary e-mail to set the frame. So, if I'm starting out an e-mail with "just see yourself (doing whatever)," I'm setting the frame to visual. Then, if the sales page continues the visual trance, I'm communicating.

Another point worth mentioning is that most people have tapes running in their heads constantly.

In sales, the tape we're up against says, "What's in it for me?"

It's auditory, and it's loud. There are other tapes that you can postulate, but that's the one that's loudest.

There's a skepticism that jaded readers bring to a sales page that assumes that the sales page is for the benefit of the person selling the item.

To knock that frame off and reset with a buying frame (to the reader's benefit), I've learned to start out with the answer to those questions.

Copywriters know to stress the benefits right at the top of the page—but they don't always tell you why. It's been my experience that if you can join the reader's conversation with him/herself, you can quickly communicate.

Reader: *What's in it for me?*

Copywriter: *You're gonna look so good driving this sports car.*

Reader: *What's in it for me?*

Copywriter: *You can keep your money in your pocket. This car is maintenance free.*

Reader: *What's in it for me?*

Copywriter: *The first 100 people who buy this car will go down in history, and will receive publicity far more valuable than the price of the car. They will also be perceived as intelligent and sexy, and there's a very good chance that owning this car will get you real close to Lindsay Lohan.*

Reader: *Where can I get it?*

So, if you can postulate or control the self-talk in readers, you can join their conversation and reset the frame to bring them into the sales copy—an important first step.

Dave Lakhani, author of *Persuasion: The Art of Getting What You Want* and *Power of an Hour*, said:

One of the most effective ways of eliciting the state that people are in is to ask very specific questions; in fact, the more specific the question, the higher the quality of information you'll get back. So rather than taking their first answer, I ask more exacting questions, questions like:

How will or how do you define that?

How do you know?

What made you draw that conclusion?

Tell me more about that. . . .

Can you explain that to me?

What is an example of how this might work, be true. or where someone has used it?

By asking detailed questions, you get many specific answers that will give you clues as to what people are really thinking, where they have drawn their conclusions, and who has influenced their thinking. They will also expose the weaknesses in their thinking or their illusions. Once you know those things you are in a much better position to deepen their trance by adding congruency (agreeing, leading, etc.) or to do a pattern interrupt by disagreeing or by abruptly shifting the course of the conversation.

A way of knowing what people are thinking is to draw them out. Fake psychics who practice cold reading do this all the time. They present generalities as observations of fact, allow the person to respond to them, and then mold their conversation around them. Some good examples of that are statements like these, which work to pull people out in virtually any situation and make you appear to be very insightful.

"You appear to me to be a person who is an independent thinker and doesn't accept others' opinions without strong evidence of truth."

"At the end of the day, it seems like you have a great deal of un-used capacity that is going to be channeled into something even more meaningful and creative."

"You prefer a little change and variety, and when corralled by restrictions, limitations, or small thinking, you become dissatisfied."

By making observations about people that feel comfortable, you enter their reality of themselves and become a part of their reality. Once you are a part of their reality, you can then impact their reality. You can deepen the trance or change the focus of the trance. Advertisers do this all the time by "mind reading" their prospects. They in effect create the trance by saying: "You are like me, and as we act together we are smarter, and you may begin to notice that only successful people or beautiful people or smart people or financially secure people (narrowing their focus) do these things and because you are that, you should do it, too (social proof)."

But, by mind reading, what you are really doing is getting them to lower their critical thinking filters, their resistance to your information because you demonstrated great insight. This is in fact exactly why people walk around in a trance all the time, and it often takes a giant sledgehammer blow to their reality to shake them out of it.

However, sometimes the most profitable move is to leave them there and deepen their trance, make their self-induced state their reality, and allow them to experience it more and more as real (a key trance-deepening technique in hypnosis—"You may feel the air in your nose, you may become aware of your chest rising and falling, you may notice when you drive the new Porsche that women seem *more interested and attentive") because the more real the trance becomes, the more lucid the hallucination, the more difficult it becomes to look at other possibilities; they just don't seem as appealing.*

Another area related to this is beliefs. People's beliefs put them into a trance nearly instantly. When they have a strong belief about something being true or not true, they rigorously defend it, they give you clear keys and clues as to what they believe ("What would Jesus do?"), or they signal nonverbally ("Vote Bush") their intentions related to their beliefs. To understand the beliefs deeply held by someone is to be able to deeply influence and persuade them. In order for beliefs to continue, they must be supported by a complementary group. So that group of like-minded people (all creating their own trance) begin to act as one, and as the group goes, so goes the individual.

Storytelling and metaphor are the gateways to creating effective buying trances because they impact people at a subconscious level—people instantly understand what to do and how to react when they hear a story. Notice the change in your own body and physiology now when I say, "When I was a boy, I grew up in a cult. I was raised to believe . . ." Your whole physiology shifts and I can take it in any direction I want at that point. I can create intense curiosity or I can transfer the state by creating a moral that says, "If you believe X then imagine Y, and it, too, is true."

Metaphor, while more complicated for people to create, is much easier for the brain to grasp and interpret. It also has the benefit of being a Buying Trance posthypnotic suggestion. The moment you hear the metaphor you have the experience. Metaphor is also a trigger.

In order to use either storytelling or metaphor to create a Buying Trance, you simply need to think about where people are at with their belief systems and with their current trances and enter their construct. When there is no commonality for you to mirror, then you enter their construct by telling a story about your product or service, because when you do, they go into a preprogrammed trance, one in which they listen intently without critical thinking filters and react emotionally. *They know that stories elicit their emotions and they know how to respond (buy) when the moral of your story leads them to their own most logical conclusion, which happens to be one you share (much more effective than the old sales close).*

Mark J. Ryan, author, therapist, salesman, and trainer of hypnosis and neuro-linguistic programming (NLP) (www .markjryan.com), said:

Someone once told me that the developers of NLP, Richard Bandler and John Grinder, had a running argument. One of them believed that everyone was in a trance 24/7 and the other said that we are never in a trance—or something like that. Well, I believe the one who said we are always in a trance. I always presume people are always in some kind of trance . . . some longer than others, some more intense, many overlapping. Richard Bandler also said to me once that "without curiosity NLP wouldn't exist."

And I say if you stay curious when encountering someone already in a trance you can begin to find out what their present trance is and then lead them into a buying trance.

There are several different ways I like to do this from a curious trance state that I get into. Yes, that's right: You, too, must enter trances to gain the trust and rapport you will need for the customer to trust you with his or her trance.

Get out of your ego trance.

Get out of your know-it-all trance.

Get out of your "I know what they need" trance.

Get out of your trance as much as possible and get into their trance.

People's favorite subject is themselves, so get curious about their favorite subject.

So what do you do when you are in a curious state to find out where they are?

If you are in retail and the customer is approaching you . . . I always make comments about what they are looking at. I do it in a statement and not in a question form. I know that I like my space when looking for retail products. A statement doesn't infringe on me like a question does, so I afford the same courtesy.

I will keep making statements such as "Those sunglasses are brand-new." "They have an amazing lens." "You can actually see 15 percent sharper with that lens." What I am doing is giving them some time to determine if they want to engage. I am respecting that they may want to stay in their present trance. I make statements because then they don't have to speak if they don't want to.

If I sense they don't want to engage, I may say something to the point of "You seem to be deep in thought," again a statement meant to draw them out. If they look interested . . . and are not talking, then I will ask a question such as "What are you thinking about using the glasses for?" Now I get an idea of where they are and can work from there.

If someone is in a hurry I might say to them, "you seem in a hurry." The answer is yes or no and if they are, I follow up with another question of "Is there anything I can help you with to get you on your way?"

People will usually be polite at this point and say something like "I am going out on a boat with friends in five minutes and I need a pair of sunglasses." So now I know the trance they are thinking about and I enter into how I might feel if I were in that same situation and pace them into a Buying Trance for my product only if it will be of value to them.

In other situations besides retail, I might still make statements, and would be ready to engage them with questions sooner.

I get curious about what they may be wearing, what their office is decorated with, and the theme that might interest them enough for them to put up those certain things. What kind of car are they driving? What restaurant are we meeting at? What kind of sports are they interested in?

The point is you must find a "close trance"—a trance that is close at all times to whatever trance they may be in at the time.

Because you usually cannot just ask for their present trance—most people will not reveal that and will want to get away from you ASAP—you find a close trance that they can easily access without much effort. "Is that a Red Sox pin on your lapel?" Either way, yes or no, you now have a close trance to work from. If it is not a Red Sox pin the person may say, "No, it is a hole-in-one pin from my country club, Red Stone." Hey, you were wrong, but look at the juicy information you just got, and who wouldn't or couldn't be curious about a hole in one? And how hard is it going to be to get the person to talk about a hole in one? And how many different points of interest might come from that story?

And a very neat thing is that once you get into a close trance and make that a "present trance," you can go in many different directions from there to get to the Buying Trance.

There is no perfect way to do this; however, the more you develop your own style using these ideas, the quicker you will find people openly sharing their present trances. People seem to sense that you are genuinely curious and interested in them, sometimes without saying a word to them. I don't know how many times people have said to me, "I cannot believe I am telling you this—I don't even know you." I smile and they continue on.

People like to buy from people they like. People like people who show interest in them.

Get curious . . . but not too curious. :-)

John Burton (www.drjohnburton.com), therapist and author of *Hypnotic Language*, said:

How do I get an inkling of what another person is feeling or thinking or experiencing in their inner world? In my work as a psychotherapist I need to understand what my client is experiencing inside his or her mind. Clients and people in general provide some clues as to what they think or feel in the natural process of communicating. During my training in neuro-linguistic programming (NLP), I was taught about modes of communicating. In this case, modes refer to the adjectives a person uses when speaking. Maybe when someone talks to you, you hear references to one of the five senses. "I just think that stinks!" or "Man, that leaves a really bad taste in my mouth!" or "Wow, what a sweet deal!" Other examples on the positive side might be, "That has a good ring to it" or "I can see how that will work well."

People often utilize one of their five senses when selecting words to convey particular meaning. This selected sense can give you some insight into how people process and make sense of information in their world. NLP shows that by speaking back to people in the same sense they used in speaking to you, a better and more effective connection occurs. But here, I want to speak of another way of knowing using a different set of pathways.

In the course of communicating with another person, the sender will often utilize one or more senses in sending information. Some people use their hands when they speak and some people just move their body more in general when speaking or when listening. Other people make vigorous facial expressions when communicating. Still others are nearly poker-faced while talking or listening. These modes of communicating provide ports of entry into the other person's world. This port of entry can lead to what might be termed trance sharing.

We each live a high percentage of our lives in a trance, experiencing some narrow focus that excludes alternative items or views. It is tricky for us humans to expand our awareness and consider multiple concepts at one time. And yet this still qualifies as a trance as well. So in some sense we spend most of our time in a trance, fixing our awareness on something. Communicating, in some ways, simply involves a person describing to another person or persons the trance he or she is experiencing. Wow! What about that movie you saw last weekend, sharing your trance experience with others as you describe the movie to them. Oh boy, that vegetable garden is in-

credible! You should see just how red and ripe and huge those toma-
toes are this year! When you see your neighbor's tomatoes in your
head, you are trance sharing. Hmmm, maybe they need a little wa-
ter in there?

And so now to answer the question posed by Joe. How do I see
my neighbor's red, ripe tomatoes in my head before they tell me?
How do I know what they think or feel about those fine tomatoes?
Each person tends to favor an avenue of communicating, whether it
is body movement, facial expressions, or just words and tone of
voice. Detecting the sender's most prominent mode can allow you to
trance-share, providing you with inside information about the
sender's thoughts or emotions.

The first step in trance sharing is acknowledging that whoever is
communicating to you is already in a trance. They have something
on their mind about which they are in a trance.

Utilizing this, step 2 is inviting the other person to describe
their trance to you in detail. These details allow the person to share
their trance with you. As they describe their trance content to you
they invariably rely on their strongest communication suit. Maybe
this involves hand and body movement, maybe it involves their fa-
cial expressions or maybe it is just a methodical streaming verbal
presentation.

In any case, for step 3 I tune into their format and try it on. I
empathize as much as I can so that I experience what and how
they speak to me. I imagine my hands moving that way and no-
tice my resulting thoughts and what emotions occur. I imagine
experiencing their facial expression and just feel what I feel and
observe any thoughts coming to mind. If the person presents in a
sort of strictly verbal mode then I listen carefully and try on the
words and the tone and the pace, allowing thoughts and feelings
to occur.

Step 4 involves the beginning of a more fully shared trance. I
may see pictures of their descriptions. I may just hear words that
they then use. When I see or hear their details as they do or just in
advance of their sharing out loud, then I know I'm in with them.

The fifth step becomes where therapy happens. Here I look around their world and see alternative points of view and influencing factors in the present situation. I can then reverse the order of trance sharing. I share my alternative trance with the client, providing alternative perceptions, thoughts, emotions, and behaviors. A new, yet more effective and resourceful, trance begins for the client out of their choice from the additional alternatives noticed.

Finally, an interesting approach to determine what people are thinking is from copywriter Sam Rosen of www.verticalitygroup.com. He said:

I look primarily to Ken Wilber's AQAL model, based on his integral theory, to understand buying trances. With AQAL (all quadrants, all levels, as well as all lines, all states, and all types), we learn that every experience contains four dimensions: the interior-individual, the exterior-individual, the interior-collective, and the exterior-collective.

In other words, when I'm thinking about a prospect, I run through a checklist in my mind:

1. *What aspects of the prospect's worldviews, psychological composition, and inner experiences of consciousness (interior-individual) define their reasons for looking at this product?*

2. *What behavioral and physical issues does the prospect care about (exterior-individual)?*

3. *What values systems make up the prospect's cultural environment and social milieu (interior-collective)?*

4. *What kind of business is the prospect in, how is it structured, and what role does the prospect see the company playing in society at large and humanity's ongoing development (exterior-collective)?*

The previous four questions represent each quadrant. But within each quadrant, there are levels, lines, states, and types.

Let's focus on the first question: the inner dimensions of the individual. Now, that individual might feel incredibly stressed all of the time—disconnected, depressed, lacking any real sense of purpose or passion. In other words, she is experiencing repeated state of distress. I can simply observe her state from tone of voice, nonverbal cues, and, in many cases, lifestyle.

Now, even though that person is in a stressed-out state, she might be very intellectually sophisticated and morally evolved— and yet, she clearly has a difficult time handling her emotions. These various areas of development—intellectual, moral, emotional (and spiritual, cognitive, etc.)—are called lines.

If a prospect needs work on her emotional development but is intellectually quite sophisticated, then her Buying Trance might sound something like: "I need emotional help, but I also need intellectual stimulation, a clear sense of ethics and authenticity, perhaps a tinge of the cutting edge and empirical reasoning behind why your product works."

This is where it gets fun. Each of those lines—moral, intellectual, emotional, spiritual, and so on—can actually develop. So, for instance, I might have an incredible intellect, but I have neither spiritual awareness nor moral standards. I'm sure you know some people like that! They're smart, yes, but they just can't cope with life. And at the same time, I once knew someone who taught enlightenment and had read every spiritual book on the block, but he ended up going to jail for stealing money. He had access to spiritual states of consciousness, but his levels of development in the moral and ethical lines were quite low.

The list of human complexities goes on—you can probably see how this could go on forever—and my responsibility as an integral marketer is to understand how all of these factors produce a specific Buying Trance in the individual and to position the product in a way, using hypnotic storytelling, that leads to the highest possible good for all involved.

The marketplace is essentially a combination of the myriad levels, lines, states, and types that exist in each of the four quadrants. Each target market—and, at the micro level, each prospect—manifests identifiable patterns within the AQAL model. Understand this, and the reasons why people buy what they buy starts to make a lot more sense. For more on integral theory and the AQAL model, check out Ken Wilber's classic, A Brief History of Everything.

———

The point of this chapter is to give you a few ways to begin to x-ray your prospect's mind. The more you can understand his or her current trance, the better you can take control and create the Buying Trance.

THE STORY OF THE PORTABLE EMPIRE

Even though I am the father of the Buying Trance, it doesn't mean I have the technique down pat just yet. I still slip up. I'm still learning. I'm still reminding myself that I put people into a Buying Trance only when I focus on *them*, not on me or what I want to sell. I also know that how I direct them to do something will determine what they actually do. My words create the beginning of their mind-set, which leads to the action they take. With that in mind, let me confess the following story, which will also teach you more about the inner workings of the Buying Trance.

MY GOOF

In 2006 Pat O'Bryan, one of my business partners and a dear friend, released his long-awaited CD and DVD set called *Your Portable Empire*. I was excited about it. I wanted to drive traffic to his web site and see the sales roll in. Because I loved his

site, and particularly the graphic at the top of the site, I wrote
the following e-mail and sent it to my list:

Subject: What may be the greatest web site of all time?

Pat O'Bryan just sent me a link to look at his new web site.
   I wasn't interested.
   I was tired, just on a teleseminar, and didn't want to go
look.
   But it was for Pat, so I did.
   And it fried me.
   The graphic at the very top not only made me smile, but
the words on it have to be the greatest summary of an
irresistible offer I've ever seen online.
   I don't care if you're busy, or tired, or what. You simply
have to go look. It won't take but a sec. It's at http://snipurl
.com/unseminar or www.marketerschoice.com/
app/?Clk=1507703.
   Go see.
   Joe
PS—If you want to create your own Portable Empire, which is
what Pat is known for, then get your rear to
http://snipurl.com/unseminar.

I sent the e-mail and waited.
And waited.
Sales receipts did not burst into my e-mail box. Although
my e-mail created traffic to Pat's site, there were no sales. I
found this very perplexing.
As it happened, famous Internet marketer Mark Joyner
sent me an e-mail to say hi. Mark is the author of *The Great
Formula* and *The Irresistible Offer*. He's a genius at online marketing and the key person who helped me promote myself
online with my first e-books almost 10 years ago.
I told Mark about my e-mail and the lack of results. He

surprised me by pointing out that my framing was all wrong. He said by driving people to look at the site to study a graphic, I sent people to the site with the wrong end in mind. They needed to be going with an urge to buy, not just with a desire to look. In short, I was thinking of myself and my own interests, and not the prospect and his or her interests.

In other words, I created the perception in the reader's mind that the site was worth study, which meant they went there to study it. But what I needed to do was put in their minds that the site contained *benefits for them*, which would lead them to get to the site with a completely different mind-set.

With Mark's lesson in mind, I wrote this follow-up e-mail and sent it to my list:

Subject: I goofed—and you can learn from my mistake.

I sent out an e-mail yesterday urging you to see one of the best web sites I've seen in a long time at http://snipurl.com/ unseminar.

Many of you went, but not all of you bought.

When I mentioned it to Mark Joyner, he said my positioning was all wrong.

He explained that by having you go to look at the site, you didn't go to look at the benefits of the product.

In other words, I violated one of my own principles of how to lead someone to buy.

Mark said I should have focused on all you get, such as—

- You learn how to set up your own online business in 30 days or less.
- You learn about hypnotic writing, hypnotic marketing, hypnotic publicity, and much more.
- You learn the quick-start secrets for building a moneymaking business.

You get the idea.

Because I sent you to the site to look at the hypnotic graphic, you went there with a mind-set to learn about hypnotic graphics.

There was nothing wrong with that, except I also wanted you to go *buy*.

This is the lesson: Whenever you want to get someone to do something, how you lead them there will determine what they do.

I led you to look.

But I needed to lead you to buy.

So let me try again.

Please go review Pat's site because the product he offers can put you into business—and making money—with your own Portable Empire in about 30 days.

If Pat—a once-struggling musician with several CDs out but always broke—can do it, then so can you.

See http://snipurl.com/unseminar.

In one of my next mailings, I'll send you the e-mail you should have gotten in the first place. But don't let that stop you from reviewing his site.

Go for it.

Joe

PS—This very e-mail ought to prove that nobody knows it all (except maybe Mark Joyner). If I can still learn something new, then so can you. Get Pat's package and get to the head of the class. Go see http://snipurl.com/unseminar.

This new e-mail drove even more traffic to the web site, which now began to lead to sales. It also had a secondary benefit: People respected the fact that I—an alleged Internet marketing guru—admitted a mistake and confessed I could still learn something from another. This increased my credibility with readers, which of course made it easier for people to trust what I said.

And just in case you're curious, here's the final e-mail I sent to promote Pat's product. You'll notice that this one focuses on what is *currently on the mind of the reader*, which is the number one thing to do to begin a genuine Buying Trance:

Subject: The problem (and three solutions)

The number one question I hear from people is, "Where do I begin?"

They hear about all the courses promising to reveal how to make it big online, and they are confused. They wonder—

Which one works?

Who do you believe?

Where do I begin with any of them?

I can understand the problem. After all, it seems like everyone—and his brother (and sister)—is hyping some new course. Some of these gurus I've heard of and personally know. Some I don't know at all.

If I were just starting out online, I'd be confused, too.

So what's a well-meaning newbie to do?

The way I see it, there are three ways to handle this problem of confusion and indecision. They are—

1. Wing it.

    Just jump in. Try everything, and see what works. This approach takes time, energy, pesos, and commitment, but you could do it. This might be the ticket for you. There are stories of babes in the online woods who try something new and strike gold in cyberspace. Anything is possible.

    I just can't help but think results would come quicker with just a little guidance, which leads me to...

2. Get mentored.

    Everyone needs a coach, at least in some areas of their life and business. If you want to look into this, the group I endorse is the one that conducts my own Executive Mentoring Program. You can get details at www.northstarmentoring.com. But mentoring can be relatively expensive, and that's why I also suggest . . .

3. Build a Portable Empire.

This is what you ultimately want. The man who created his own Portable Empire in record time is the same man today teaching others how to do it. Get his course. It guarantees to show you how to set up your own online "empire" in 30 days or less.

Pat O'Bryan was a struggling musician who quickly cut his teeth online and is now a guru to the newbies following behind him. He understands the beginner's mind. His program speaks right to you.

After all, he was once sitting at home reading an e-mail much like this one, asking himself, "Where do I begin?"

In his case, he attended my now-famous Spiritual Marketing Seminar in Austin, Texas. He learned what he needed and took off like a cyber-rocket. All I could see was his smoke.

A while back Pat held his own seminar to help people who wanted to do well online but didn't have a clue where to start or what to do. He recorded it all, and describes it all at http://snipurl.com/unseminar.

His huge package of CDs and DVDs is a complete, paint-by-the-numbers approach to making it online.

He and his speakers (I was one of them) take you by the hand and guide you in building your own online business—from scratch.

See http://snipurl.com/unseminar for details.

Or www.marketerschoice.com/app/?Clk=1507703.

There you have it: three solutions to one problem.

All you have to do is choose one.

In truth, you could probably do all three solutions:

1. Get Pat's course.

2. Get mentoring to help you implement it.

3. Be creative in what you try.

Whatever you decide, it's up to you to make it so.
If you don't take action, who will?
Go for it.
Joe

PS—Pat is offering a staggering list of bonuses for the next group of people who order his package. See http://snipurl .com/unseminar for details. (His site is well worth a visit, if only to admire the graphic at the top of the page.)

As you can see from that final e-mail, I now put the graphic—which was the entire focus of the first e-mail—as a *final* comment. This caused people to go to the site with a completely different perception: to learn how to make money online, which tied in to *their* interests, as well as to one of Roy Garn's "fatal four" emotional appeals.

This story illustrates a point made by Tom Stafford and Mike Webb in their book, *Mind Hacks*: "Attention acts like a kind of filter, directing all resources to certain tasks and away from others."

How you lead someone to anything frames the attention they will give to do the task. In my first e-mail for Pat's package, I created an awareness to pay attention to a graphic. Well, that attention doesn't allow for a Buying Trance. By the time I sent out the third e-mail, I was creating an awareness of the value of the product. That new focus leads people into a Buying Trance.

GET OUT OF YOUR EGO

In short, when you write anything or speak to your prospects, you have to always keep their interests in mind. You have to relentlessly focus on what they will get from your pitch. In fact, you should drop the word *pitch* from your volcabulary. Instead, just keep thinking "You will get . . ." when talking or writing to a prospect.

The bottom line is this: Get out of your ego and into your prospect's ego. The more you can do that, the better and faster will be the Buying Trance you create.

CONVERSATIONAL TRANCES: THE FOUR STATES OF MIND

Not all of your marketing or sales will be in print or over the air, so you should also be aware of how face-to-face Buying Trances work. To understand this aspect of this new psychology of sales and marketing, you need to be aware of the four states of mind. They are: beta, alpha, theta, and delta.

If you've studied meditation, hypnosis, or psychology, you've probably heard of these states of mind before. Here are quick definitions for each:

1. **Beta:** Normal awake state, busy, many thoughts, active mind.

2. **Alpha:** Daydreaming or relaxed focused, meditative.

3. Theta: Deep trance, inspirational.

4. Delta: Asleep. No conscious awareness.

In this chapter you'll learn how people can enter a Buying Trance in conversation. The same principles apply, but the look and feel is different. Let's take a look.

TALKING TRANCE

How do the four states of mind look when brought to life outside of a therapy session and in the business meeting room?

When you talk to most people, they are in the beta state. Their minds are busy—alive with things to do, concerns, worries, and much more. Imagine a room full of kindergarten kids all playing, talking, and fighting and you have a mental image of the beta state in most people. When you try to talk to them, you are trying to get a room of brats to settle down.

When you talk to some people, especially if they are relaxed, such as lounging by a pool with a drink in hand, they may be in an alpha state of mind. Depending on what you say, you may be able to easily get their attention and hold it. They don't have as much going on in their heads.

Unless you're a hypnotist, you'll probably never have a conversation with someone in a theta or delta state. You wouldn't want one, anyway. They will be very quiet and withdrawn.

From those four descriptions, it should be clear you want to get people into an alpha state of mind. Considering the hustle and bustle of today's high-stress, high-tech, always-busy world, that may seem impossible. It isn't.

THE SECRET

When I was a journalism student at Kent State University back in the 1970s, I learned a trick to get people to relax.

Whenever I or any reporter has to interview someone, the person being interviewed is on guard. They may not be expecting something bad, but they are expecting to be recorded. They clam up. They watch what they say because they don't want to look foolish. Who can blame them, right?

But I was always able to get subjects to relax by asking one question. All I would do was say, "What do you do for fun or relaxation?"

Although I didn't know it when I was a youth in college, I was hypnotically leading people to relax. By asking them what they did to relax, they had to go to that place within where they knew the state called relaxation.

For example, I remember one of my first interviews. I was just as nervous as the grizzly old professor I interviewed. But I began by asking him what he did for relaxation. To my surprise, he relaxed. He began to tell me about his golf game. I didn't know a thing about golf. I'd never played it. But I listened. As I showed attention, my interviewee told me stories. He was very proud of a hole in one he scored one day. It was also my first time to know what a "hole in one" meant.

The point is, my single question turned an awkward moment into a rapport-building one. This story illustrates how you might capture people's attention—and begin a Buying Trance—by focusing on their likes, not yours.

But what if you come across a difficult prospect?

HOW TO HANDLE RESISTANT PROSPECTS

W hat if you come across people who are resistant to your sales message?

What if you approach someone who seems interested but remains skeptical?

What if you hit a brick wall before you even open your mouth?

There is a solution. It comes from the world of hypnotherapy and was invented by one of the most powerful and innovative hypnotists and therapists of recent history.

Milton Erickson, the famous hypnotherapist, invented a form of hypnotic therapy called the "naturalistic approach." It was basically hypnosis without an induction. In other words, Erickson didn't spend time asking you to relax or close your eyes, or do any other obvious or formal form of trance induction. Instead, Erickson simply talked to you. He would use whatever you said or whatever he noticed about you, and weave it into an apparent conversation. That conversation would more often than not put you into a trance state.

Erickson was able to use his naturalistic or utilitarian approach to handle the most resistant clients. He didn't always cure the chronic cases, but his success rate was still higher than that of most therapists. According to *The Wisdom of Milton H. Erickson* by Ronald Havens, one definition of Erickson's approach is this: "Use whatever dominant beliefs, values, attitudes, emotions, or behaviors the patient presents in order to develop an experience that will initiate or facilitate therapeutic change."

I believe we can model Erickson's "no induction" healing process to the sales and marketing world. When you have to deal with prospects who are resistant to your sales message, and even when you are approaching someone open but skeptical about your offer, this heart approach to sales and marketing can make all the difference to your bottom line.

If we translate the definition of Erickson's method into marketing terms, it might look like this: "Use whatever dominant beliefs, values, attitudes, emotions, or behaviors the prospect presents in order to develop an experience that will initiate or facilitate the Buying Trance."

Let's see how this might work.

MILTON ERICKSON'S THREE STEPS

Milton Erickson used a three-step process to implement his naturalistic approach to change. Here are his three steps, from a therapist's view, according to Yvonne Dolan in her book, *A Path with a Heart*:

1. "The therapist must accept and appreciate the problematic resistant behavior or perception as a legitimate piece of communication from the client regarding the client's current inner state and the client's model of the world."

2. "The therapist must be willing to view the client's problematic resistant behavior or perception as a potentially valuable therapeutic resource."

3. "The therapist must communicate this acceptance and appreciation to the client in an undeniable way."

I'll translate the three steps into sales and marketing terms:

1. No matter what your prospects say or do, it is a valid expression *from their point of view.*

2. You must accept their point of view as a *potential sales tool.*

3. You must agree with their point of view *sincerely.*

Once you discover the simple power in these three steps, you are well on the way to knowing how to create powerful and instant Buying Trances to handle resistant prospects. Here's a quick story to illustrate how this might work.

MEETING RESISTANCE

Imagine this.

One day you call on a potential client. He or she sounds out of breath. Instead of trying to dive into your sales pitch, you ask what's wrong. The prospect begins to tell you about their day. They are not about to listen to you talk about your widget. They are stressed and distracted. You could excuse yourself and call back later. Or you could try the following.

Whatever they say, acknowledge it and even agree with it. Don't talk them out of it. Don't argue with them. Accept their view of their current reality as true. After all, it *is* true, based on their thoughts in this moment. If you could switch places with them and be in their shoes in this moment, you'd probably feel as they do.

As you listen, you have the quiet knowing that where this prospect is in their mind is a useful tool to make a later sale.

So you genuinely accept it, not trying to change them at all. You continue listening, maybe asking questions to better understand where the person is coming from.

You agree with their point of view. After you've heard their explanation for it, you *should* agree with it, at least from an intellectual understanding. By agreeing that whatever they are experiencing is valid, you create rapport. It's this state of rapport that creates the beginning of a Buying Trance. It's this rapport that melts resistance. People don't like to feel alone. They want someone on their side. A friend is easier to buy from than a salesperson or marketer. Be a friend.

The process doesn't stop there, of course. Even Milton Erickson would build on what he heard *after* rapport was established to lead the client out of his or her current trance. But you can't take someone into a new trance without merging or breaking their existing one. Erickson was a master at merging with a trance before leading into a new one. When it comes to working with resistant prospects, agreeing with them is a wiser strategy than arguing with them.

Agreement melts resistance.

Agreement leads to trance.

Agreement leads to sales.

THE 10-SECOND TRANCE INDUCTION

If people are already in a preoccupied state of mind when you approach them in person, or on the phone, or with a sales letter or brochure, how do you get them out of their current trance and into your Buying Trance—and in under 10 seconds?

The secret is in getting their attention fast. A stage hypnotist can put a person in a trance within minutes, sometimes seconds, sometimes with a handshake or with the right word spoken at the right time. There's a special dynamic going on in that situation, of course. The people at the show are *expecting* to go into a trance, so the hypnotist has an easier job.

Brad Fallon is a search engine optimization (SEO) expert and great guy. I got to know him on the marketing cruise I was on in 2005, when we were both speakers. After our presentations, we hung out together and picked each other's brains. He asked me about my P. T. Barnum book, *There's a*

Customer Born Every Minute, writing in general, and hypnosis, too. Brad wanted to know if it was true that a hypnotist could put someone into a trance just by shaking the person's hand.

I told him, yes, of course. Stage hypnotists do it all the time. They have to learn instant inductions in order to make the show happen fast. Milton Erickson was famous for being able to put people into a trance state with a handshake, too. I told Brad I could do it, as well, and I stretched out my hand.

He offered his hand to mine but just as we touched, he quickly realized what could happen and pulled his hand away. We both laughed but the point was made. The *expectation* that something as innocent as a handshake could put you into a hypnotic trance is exactly what makes it possible.

Here's another example: Harry Carpenter, in his book *The Genie Within,* writes of a PBS television show where a volunteer was asked to *pretend* to be hypnotized. The instructor on the program did nothing else to create a trance—no inductions, no guided relaxations, no staring at a swinging watch. Yet the volunteer went into an apparent trance. To test the mind of the volunteer, the instructor handed him a Spanish onion but told him it was an apple. The volunteer ate the onion, thinking and acting as if it were an apple. Yet the entire instant trance was done by suggesting the subject pretend he was in a trance!

Obviously, trance states—even instant ones—are real, and very powerful.

A HYPNOTIC E-STUNT

To give you another example of how instant hypnosis works, I once hypnotized Mark Joyner while thousands of people listened to it happen. Mark is the author of several books, including *The Great Formula* and *The Irresistible Offer.* To help promote one of our mutual products, I came up with the idea of hypnotizing Mark live, on a teleseminar, as a publicity stunt to get everyone's attention.

The hypnosis was very real. I spoke to Mark on the phone, before the actual live event, to prep him for the experience. Since Mark has known me for many years, and is in fact the man who released my first e-book, *Hypnotic Writing*, many years ago, he is well aware of my hypnotic abilities. I further enforced his understanding that I knew hypnosis by reminding him that I speak at the yearly convention for hypnotists, the National Guild of Hypnotists. I also sent out e-mails promoting the live event by saying, "I can hypnotize anyone who is willing in under three minutes." Of course, Mark got to see those e-mails. They helped reinforce my ability to put anyone—even Mark—into a trance.

When the time came to hypnotize him, it was easy. He was prepped for it. He *expected* it. He went into a trance and stayed there until I bought him out of it. We had a record-breaking turnout for our teleseminar. We also made history, as I was the first person in Internet history to hypnotize someone live in cyberspace.

In case you are wondering, the hypnosis session was innocent. I asked him questions about his life, how he first got started online, and more. I wasn't conducting a stage hypnosis show where I asked a participant to do something silly for the entertainment of the crowd. I instead focused on using hypnosis to get a famous Internet marketer to tell the truth about his life and work. Since Mark always tells the truth, the hypnosis session didn't reveal much new. But it still drew a crowd. And people are still talking about it today. Even Mark.

But what about you and me, when we approach a prospect cold?

How do you get their attention and hold it?

It's still possible to get someone's attention quickly. You can do it within seconds if you do it right. And when you do it right, it could mean an abundance of sales.

All of this was proven in the 1930s by a man known for selling the sizzle, not the steak.

TESTED SELLING INSTITUTE

Elmer Wheeler founded the Tested Selling Institute back in the 1930s. He wrote many books, such as *Tested Sentences That Sell* and *Word Magic*. Wheeler proved that people have a mental window of 10 seconds. If you don't grab their attention in 10 seconds, they will go back to their current trance and tune you out.

Wheeler's method was to write dozens of word combinations, or Tested Selling Sentences, for any product he was trying to promote. He then tested them all, either on friends or, if the client would stand for it, on customers, until he found the perfect phrase.

In one 10-year period he tested 105,000 sentences for 5,000 products. He eliminated just about 100,000 sentences. For example, in seeking the sizzle in Barbasol, he tested 141 sentences. He finally selected: "How would you like to cut your shaving time in half?" This boosted Barbasol sales 300 percent.

When Texaco needed a sales kick, Wheeler studied gas stations and noticed the clerks were asking, "Check your oil today?" Wheeler came up with the more hypnotic question, "Is your oil at the proper level today?" For these eight words, Texaco paid Wheeler $5,000. This was $625 a word in the 1930s—the time of Depression-era America.

Wheeler worked out the malted-milk-and-egg technique for Abraham & Straus, so that the stores might sell more eggs at their soda fountains. He not only devised the phrase "One or two eggs today?" but also planned the gesture of the clerk holding an egg in each hand.

In each situation Wheeler devised a fast attention-getting statement to grab a person from the trance they were in and get them into his trance, which usually led to a sale. As Wheeler pointed out in his famous talk, "Magic Words That Make People Buy":

> You have only 10 short seconds in which to catch the fleeting interest of the other person, and if in those short 10 seconds you

don't say something mighty important, that prospect is going to leave you mentally if he has not already left you physically.

When you approach anyone in any way, you have a bare 10 seconds to get them out of their trance state. One way to approach them is what I described in the preceding chapter: you join them by agreeing with them. But another approach is to jolt them, pleasantly, out of their trance long enough for you to get them focused on your message.

Here's how to do it.

PITCH AND GROW RICH

"Step right up!"

That's the call of the carnival barker and the subtle command of the infomercial host. It works virtually every time, too. People line up to buy $1 mice that move by magic, as well as exercise equipment that costs hundreds of dollars— only to be used as a clothes hanger later.

The secret art of the pitchmen has been used to sell Ginzu knifes, Pocket Fishermen, Potato Guns, Steam Magic, D-Frost Wonders, and Topsy Tail Hair Curlers. None of these items are essential to life, yet people spend their hard-earned money to buy them.

How is this possible? What do pitchmen on television or in the fairs know that we don't? How are they able to grab and hold attention, and then get people to part with their money when they were never in a buying mood to begin with?

Pitchmen—those barkers at sideshows or trade shows— know how to get attention. They may do it with food, magic, models, displays, or any other visual or by inviting you to see whatever awaits behind the curtain.

But what about those who use *only* words to grab attention?

MAY I SEE YOUR HAND?

Nerissa and I were walking through a shopping mall one day, waiting to see a movie playing a little later in the day. As we strolled along, a young man at a center kiosk looked at Nerissa and asked, "May I see your hand for a second?"

Nerissa held out her hand. The man held it, said it was beautiful and soft, and from there Nerissa was putty in his hands. She listened as he energetically described his line of skin lotions, powders, fingernail protectors, and so on.

I didn't understand most of it. But I was mesmerized by how this complete stranger stopped us with just eight words, delivered in under 10 seconds. By the time we left his booth, we had bought $300 worth of products, including a sea salt bath and complete full-body mud pack for me!

How did this happen? While the other clerks at the other kiosks sat and waited for customers to walk up to them and say something, this enterprising young man took matters into his own hands. He invited us into his Buying Trance by doing one thing: asking a question.

WHAT STATEMENTS WORK?

If Elmer Wheeler tested 105,000 sentences on 5,000 products, you can easily imagine that finding the right question or the right statement for your audience will take some research. But here are some pointers.

Ask Open-Ended Questions

If you ask any question that can be answered with a yes or a no, chances are high the prospect will answer with a no and break the trance. Although the fellow selling skin products asked Nerissa a question that she could have said no to, it worked. He might still polish his induction with something like "How soft is your hand?"

Ask Which, Not What

This was a tip from Elmer Wheeler. He strongly advised salespeople to give customers a choice between two items being offered. "Do you want to meet on Wednesday or Friday?"

is stronger than "Do you want to meet on Friday?" Asking "Do you want large or extra-large?" presupposes someone wants a substantial order, and leads them to choose between two things you wouldn't mind selling anyway.

Ask Inward-Oriented Questions

When you ask someone to imagine something or to remember something, you send them into an internal trance state. "What would happen if you could imagine the last time you told a story and people were riveted by your message?" leads the person into a memory or trance. "Imagine closing more sales when you begin to master the Buying Trance."

Make an Unusual Claim

When my book, *The Seven Lost Secrets of Success*, first came out in 1992, I wanted to say something that would grab people's attention. My publisher, Jim Chandler, and I came up with the idea of this bold guarantee: "Use the principles in this book for six months. If you don't see a 50 percent increase in your business, we'll refund your money."

I went on one radio show, stated the guarantee, and a group of six salespeople who were listening as they drove out of town stopped, turned around, and went to the local bookstore to buy six copies of the book. My unusual claim got their attention. When you consider that these men were *leaving town* and made new plans based on my hypnotic statement, you get a sense of the power of these methods.

Dr. Marc Gitterle and I did the same thing when we announced his cholesterol-lowering natural supplement formula. We put up a web site at www.cardiosecret.com and said, "Lower your cholesterol in 30 days or your money back." This simple statement was an unusual claim, because most medical products don't come with guarantees. As a result, we grabbed people from their trance and brought them into ours.

Ask a Question They Can't Answer

I often engage my audience by telling them, "I know three words that will cause you to give me all of your money." Everyone stops. They stare. They run through their minds, wondering what the three words are. This is the same power of a trivia question. No one really cares about the answer, but the *not knowing* is something that shakes people from their current trances. In my talks, I rarely tell audiences what the three words are until the event is over—and sometimes I forget to tell them.

State Something Impossible to Believe

One of my favorite tricks is to write a headline that is so preposterous that you have to awaken from your current preoccupation and take a look at the message. I used this headline on one of my blog postings: "The Internet Was Destroyed Last Night." Obviously the Internet was not destroyed, but the wild statement got attention.

This is the same technique used by tabloids, which pull people into their stories with outrageous headlines, such as "Baby Gives Birth to Elvis" or "Cow Discovered to Be Royalty." I'm not suggesting that you write the ridiculous, but that you instead focus on the fact that your audience is preoccupied. Give them a strong headline or statement to grab their attention, and then make the statement connect to your message. For example, my blog post went on to make a very logical and stimulating point. Here it is:

The Internet Was Destroyed Last Night

I just heard that the Internet was destroyed last night.

I'm shocked, too.

I'll tell you about it in a moment, but first—

I'm reading a terrific new book called *Idealized Design*.

It's by Russell L. Ackoff, Jason Magidson, and Herbert Addison and published by Wharton School Publishing, which has been publishing some works of genius such as the earlier masterpiece, *The Power of Impossible Thinking* by Jerry Wind and Colin Crook (www .whartonsp.com).

This is another work of genius. It's basically about how to create the future for your business (or your personal life) by focusing on *what you desire* and not on what you already have.

The book reminds me of *The Attractor Factor* (www .attractorfactor.com) but with a much more corporate focus. In fact, the book's cover carries the phrase "Creating an Organization's Future."

But the principles in the book are pure *Attractor Factor* and *The Secret* (www.whatisthesecret.tv).

For example, one of their guidelines is "Focus on what you would like to have if you could have whatever you want ideally, *not* on what you do not want."

My favorite part of the whole book (so far) is where you pretend that the business you want to improve was destroyed last night.

It's gone.

Burned to the ground.

Obliterated.

Now you are in a wonderful place where you can envision how you wish the business would have been in an ideal world.

From your vision, you can work backward to figure out the steps needed to create it.

This reengineering type of concept is brought to life in the most riveting way by Russell L. Ackoff, when he opens the book by telling the story of how a CEO of Bell Laboratories walked in one day and announced, "Gentlemen, the telephone system of the United States was destroyed last night."

As a result of that announcement, which of course wasn't true, the audience was able to free their minds to go on and create what we now take for granted, such as touch-tone dialing, caller ID, speakerphones, and so on.

So—if the Internet did in fact collapse last night, how would you rebuild it?

What would your vision look like?

Ao Akua,

Joe
www.mrfire.com

Again, your audience is not thinking about you.
They are thinking of themselves.
You need a good awakener to get their attention. From there, you can lead them to the Buying Trance you want them to be in.

WHO ELSE WANTS TO WRITE A HEADLINE THAT ALWAYS WORKS?

F amed copywriter David Garfinkel teaches people how to use headlines to break the preoccupation they have or trance they are in. I interviewed David for my Hypnotic Gold membership program (www.hypnoticgold .com). He explained that because people are preoccupied with their thoughts, their lives, their problems, and more, you have to approach them carefully. Say the wrong thing and your prospect may simply turn a deaf ear or a blind eye. David said one of the best headline templates to use is this one:

"Who else wants to (fill in the blank)?"

The idea here is to "call out" your target audience with a promise of a benefit they will be glad to hear about. For example:

"Who else wants to heal their back pain?"

The words "who else" suggest others have already solved the problem. The "heal back pain" is the end result they will want. That's the formula. This format can be used in any business. The key is to remember to end it with a resulting benefit people desire. Here are a few other examples:

"Who else wants to make more sales easily?"

"Who else wants to lower their cholesterol with www.cardiosecret.com?"

"Who else wants to have younger-looking skin?"

In one of my previous books, *Hypnotic Writing*, I list 30 ways to write headlines or improve existing headlines to get attention. These are tested ways to grab people's attention when they are preoccupied, and direct them to your sales presentation. Here are three of those proven ways, to help you think about awakening people by taking them from their trance into yours:

1. *Use the word* Wanted *in your headline.*

   Everyone stops and looks to see what is wanted. It intrigues them. It stirs their curiosity. It can *begin* the process of a Buying Trance, which is the job of any hypnotic headline.

2. *Use the word* Warning *in your headline.*

   Like the word *wanted*, the word *warning* also halts people. They want to know what they are being warned about. Again, it plays on their curiosity.

3. *Use the word* Why *in your headline.*

   The word *why* begins the process of opening a person's mind. Everyone wants to know the reason behind things, even if those things seem trivial.

Before we leave this chapter, let me give you a powerful hypnotic headline that works virtually every time you use it. . . .

"GIVE ME FIVE DAYS AND—!"

Robert Collier, author of *The Robert Collier Letter Book*, wrote about a headline template he used back in the 1940s that still works today. Collier was one of the most powerful and successful sales letter writers of his generation. He's considered a legend today. His book is a masterpiece. He said:

> The "Give me 5 minutes" approach, for instance. . . . You can use it to sell relief for athlete's foot, as in—"Give me 5 days, and I'll give you relief from itching feet." Or a new dance step—"Give me 15 minutes and I'll give you the secret of dancing to the new slow-time music." Or a new car—"Give me 5 minutes and I'll give you a new sensation in riding comfort."

Try it for yourself. Pick something you want to write a sales letter about. Let's say it's an insurance service. Your headline might be:

> "Give me five minutes and I'll show you the best way to save money on your insurance."

When I taught a class on how to write your own book, one of my headlines began as follows:

> "Give me six days and I'll show you how to write your very own book."

As you can imagine, you can use this one headline as a way to generate headlines of your own.

Another famous headline that gets rephrased a lot is this one by the great copywriter John Caples, which first ran in 1925:

> "They Laughed When I Sat Down at the Piano—But When I Started To Play . . .!"

Every month I see some new variation of this one proven headline. In a recent magic magazine I even saw, "They laughed when I said I was going to be a magician—until they saw my first check!"

WHY SOME WRITING "EXPLODES" IN YOUR HEAD

The whole idea behind this secret is to learn how to adapt proven headlines and sales concepts to your own sales letters. Looking at tested, proven headlines can inspire you. Here are a few for you to chew on. See if you can determine what makes them work:

"Check the kind of body YOU want."

"Is YOUR home picture-poor?"

"How a 'Fool Stunt' Made Me a Star Salesman"

"How I Improved My Memory in One Evening"

"Why Some Foods 'Explode' in Your Stomach"

"When Doctors 'Feel Rotten' this is what they do."

"Girls . . . Want quick curls?"

"Play guitar in seven days or your money back."

"They thought I was crazy to ship LIVE MARINE LOBSTERS as far as 1,800 miles from the ocean."

"Answer these questions and work out the date of your own death."

You'll notice most successful hypnotic headlines pull people into the sales letter. They generate curiosity, as in the one about why some foods explode in your stomach. Or they ask you a question. "Do you make these mistakes in English?" was a headline so intriguing it ran unchanged for *40 years*! Or they urge you to answer their questions (as in the headline about working out the date of your own death).

The key point is this: A headline has to call out your key audience (such as "Girls . . .") and at the same time promise them a benefit that intrigues them. Do that and you're well on the way to starting a sales letter that is truly hypnotic.

And that's how you *begin* a Buying Trance.

Where do you go from the headline?

WHAT IS THE ALL-TIME BEST TRANCE INDUCER?

O n a warm, sunny day in August 1996 I knelt over the grave of P. T. Barnum and had one of the most remarkable experiences of my life.

I had begun researching the famous showman in order to write my book about his business secrets, *There's a Customer Born Every Minute*. I had visited the Barnum Museum; done research at the Historical Library in Bridgeport, Connecticut; and met with Barnum scholars, biographers, and collectors of his writings. I wanted to visit Barnum's grave and pay my respects. Little did I know that the incredible, magical experience would change my life forever.

Recently I went online to hunt for old books by some of my favorite authors. This time I went after anything by Robert Collier, mail-order advertising genius and author of such classic books as *The Secret of the Ages* and *The Robert Collier Letter Book*.

I typed in his name at one of my favorite book search engines (which I'm going to keep a secret as long as I can), and to my amazement several new (to me) titles came up. I stared wide-eyed, my mouth open, as I saw that someone had two issues of a magazine Collier edited in the late 1920s called *Mind, Inc.*

I couldn't believe it. I immediately grabbed the phone, called, and bought those magazines. A few days later they arrived.

I opened the brown package, my heart racing with excitement, and nearly drooled as I slid the little paperback-sized magazines onto my desk. They were well worn but intact. I thumbed through them and marveled at my find. Here were new articles by one of my heroes, my mentor, a man who changed my life not once but twice with his books. I felt like a happy child on Christmas morning, getting the gifts he longed for and needed most.

As I looked over the two magazines, something shifted in me. I saw an advertising technique at work that seemed hypnotic in power. I had one of those "aha!" experiences great inventors write about. I held one of the issues in my hand and read the back cover. Collier had an ad there that began—

"How can I tell if I am working aright?" many people ask.

There is an easy, simple rule. With it in front of him, not even a child could go wrong. Just ask yourself one question. If your answer is "Yes," you are on the wrong track, and you will never make much progress, until you get off it and on the right track.

If your answer is "No," then you are working in the right direction, and you have only to keep it up to attain any goal you desire.

That question is the basis of the Lesson in the next issue of "Mind, Inc." If you are looking for a road map to guide you through the mental realm, send for it!

Did you catch what Collier did?

Let me give you another example. This one comes from Collier's editorial in the opening pages of the other issue I found:

Dear Reader:

Twelve years ago, the three examining physicians at the head office of the Life Extension Institute made a thorough physical examination of the writer. They had him hop and jump and do sundry things to stir his heart into action, then they listened with their stethoscopes and nodded knowingly to each other, finally gathering in a corner to whisper earnestly together, with many a meaningful glance in the writer's direction.

The upshot of their conference was a solemn warning against all forms of violent exercise. The heart was dangerously affected, in their opinion. Tennis, horseback, swimming—all these were taboo. Even running for a street car was likely to result disastrously. If the writer wanted excitement, he might walk (as long as he did it sedately) or crawl about the floor on all fours!

That was twelve years ago, remember. A few months back, he had occasion to be examined for life insurance. The examining physician knew of the Life Extension Institute findings, so he asked the Head Examiner of his company to check his report. The Head Examiner came, made the same exhaustive heart tests as the Institute and put away his instruments with a chuckle. "When you get ready to pass out," he said, "they'll have to take out that heart and hit it with a rock to make it stop beating. Work, play, do anything you like in reason. The heart can stand anything you can!"

What made the difference? Perhaps the following lesson may give you an indication.

Collier did it again!

Did you catch his method?

Collier told you just enough to intrigue you, to get you hooked, to get you interested—and then he *stopped*!

In the first example he cleverly trapped you into wanting to know the question he kept referring to. But he never told you the question. He snared you and then asked you to send for the next lesson, where the mystery of the question would be revealed. How could anyone not send for it? I sat at my desk reading Collier's ad more than 70 years after he wrote it and I wanted to send in the coupon, too. But Collier is long dead.

I'll never know the question unless I'm lucky enough find a copy of the next issue!

In the second example Collier cleverly told you an intriguing story, asked the question that every reader would then have on his or her mind—but then didn't answer it! Again, Collier generated interest, and then told you to read the magazine to find the answer. Talk about hypnotic writing!

And that's how you get people to read your sales material. You pull them into it. You grab their attention, keep them reading, get them wanting what you have, and then—stop and tell them to send in a check or call you to get what they now so strongly desire.

Did you notice how I began this chapter? I used the Robert Collier technique to hypnotize you into reading more.

I started by saying I had an experience at Barnum's grave. What was the experience? What happened?

All of these are questions in your mind as you read the opening. It's hypnotic. And if you've read this far, you know the method works.

The next time you want to write something and be sure people actually read it, remember the Robert Collier technique. Start by writing about something that will interest the people you are addressing. Tell them an interesting story. Get them wondering about something that they want to know more about. And then *stop*. Change direction. Write about something else that may still be related to the opening, but don't resolve the opening until the end of the article—and maybe not even there. Maybe you'll want people to send in a coupon or call you for the answer. Here's an example.

I started this chapter telling you I had a memorable experience at P. T. Barnum's grave. Do you want to know what happened? Of course you do. Well, I reveal the whole astonishing story in my new book, *There's a Customer Born Every Minute.*

See how the Robert Collier technique works? You probably won't be able to sleep at night until you get my new book. Heh heh heh.

MY ULTIMATE HYPNOTIC WRITING SECRET

Here's another example of how I use the power of curiosity to motivate people to go to a web site. This is from my blog.

My Ultimate Writing Secret: An Exclusive Confession

I'm going to tell you my ultimate writing secret.

I've never revealed it before.

I'm willing to bet no other writer alive or dead ever used this method.

Shakespeare didn't do it.

Hemingway didn't do it.

Your favorite novelist or copywriter doesn't do it.

But I do.

And it's the main reason my books, sales letters, articles, e-mails, web sites, and even blog posts seem to keep people riveted to my words.

It's not the words . . . but what I am doing as I write the words.

It's one of the reasons my books become #1 best sellers and my sales letters melt down the walls of resistance in people and break all known profit records.

So here's my ultimate writing secret:

As I am writing anything—including this very blog entry—I am silently chanting three magic phrases in my mind.

I am not writing the magic phrases. You won't find them in this post. But I am saying them, silently, in the back of my mind, as I write these words to you.

If you'd like to know what the three magic phrases are, take a moment and poke your head in the door over at www.milagroresearchinstitute.com/iloveyou.htm.

Ao Akua,

Joe
www.mrfire.com

PS—I silently chanted the three magic phrases as I wrote this post and I am saying them in my mind right now as I write this PS. Can you guess what the three lines are? If so, or if not, go see www.milagroresearchinstitute.com/iloveyou.htm.

After you've read my blog entry, you should be scrambling to get to the web site mentioned in the post. You're curious. This should be obvious evidence that curiosity is one of the most powerful tools in your magic bag of tricks to get people into your Buying Trance.

And if you're *really* curious about how to use Buying Trances to get people to buy virtually anything, then just turn to the next chapter.

How to Get People to Buy Virtually Anything

How do you sell a T-shirt, anyway?

I mean, nobody really needs one. Many places give them away as promotional items. And there isn't a shortage of them in the world. They aren't food, water, or shelter. They aren't essential. No one will die without one.

So why would anyone buy one of mine?

Those were the thoughts I wrestled with after artist Andy Dooley created a beautiful T-shirt design to celebrate my book, *Life's Missing Instruction Manual*.

Now that I have a shirt, how do I sell it?

I rummaged through my brain as well as my library and stumbled across Aristotle. You may remember him. He was an ancient Greek rhetorician who created a four-point system for persuasion. That system has never been improved on in the last 2,000 years. In brief, his logical four-step "arrange-ment" (as Aristotle called it) looks like this:

1. *Exordium.* A shocking statement or story to get attention.
2. *Narratio.* You pose the problem the reader/listener is having.
3. *Confirmatio.* You offer a solution to the problem.
4. *Peroratio.* You state the benefits of action.

This should look a little familiar to you. It's very similar to the classic advertising formula known as AIDA: attention, in-terest, desire, action.

Because of both of those formulas, most of my sales-oriented writing follows along the easy path of answering these questions:

1. Are you getting attention with your opening?
2. Are you stating a problem the reader cares about?
3. Are you offering a solution that really works?
4. Are you asking the reader to take action?

Okay. You got that. But how does it help me sell T-shirts? Well, let's see.

First, my opening has to grab attention.

So what if I said something like, "How can you wear a painting that will increase your sex appeal?" Food, sex, and money are notorious attention-getters.

Second, now I have to state a problem.

So maybe I can ask, "Are you tired of wearing ratty T-shirts from the local pub or grill? Wouldn't you like to wear some-thing that makes you feel great, that reminds you—as well as the people who are attracted to you—to go for your dreams?"

Third, now I have to explain my solution.

"Famous artist Andy Dooley, who has designed T-shirts sold at Disney World and around the world, has just created an original work of art. This art is beautiful, colorful, and charged with the feelings that attract prosperity, love, and healing—all the things you loved in my book, *The Attractor Factor*."

Fourth, to wrap up, I need to now ask for action.

"You can only get this limited-edition, original work of art directly from me. Just go to my web site at www.mrfire.com and you'll see the T-shirt design. For every three shirts you buy, I'll send you one free. Sizes are Large and X-Large only."

Wow! I did it!

I spontaneously created a sales piece by following Aristotle's 2,400-year-old four-step plan.

You can do this, too. For anything you want to sell, simply ask yourself these questions:

1. Are you getting attention with your opening?
2. Are you stating a problem the reader cares about?
3. Are you offering a solution that really works?
4. Are you asking the reader to take action?

Now go and make Aristotle proud!

HOW TO CREATE
A MAGICAL
ON-THE-SPOT
BUYING TRANCE

I love magic. I'm a lifetime member of the Society of American Magicians, the organization Harry Houdini started back in the early 1900s. I know many magicians and often attend magic conventions and shows. I haunt the dealer room, where magic tricks are sold. I'm looking for the tricks that make people gasp in surprise and delight.

Unfortunately, most magic is on the level of a prank or kid's joke. That's not for me, so most magic that I see disappoints me.

But one day I met a magic dealer at a convention who was very friendly. He took his time with me, listened to my needs, and then responded with some truly hypnotic stories. Here's an example.

"I went into one of those big discount stores," Mr. Williams, the dealer, began. "The woman behind the counter seemed bored so I decided to do a little magic to liven up her day. I asked her to pretend I had a deck of cards in my hand. I then let her shuffle the make-believe cards, cut them, deal them out, and pick any card she wanted. Remember, all of this was done in her head."

Mr. Williams went on, "After I let her choose her card, I asked if she wanted to change her selection. She said no. I then announced that her card was the seven of spades."

Mr. Williams paused before telling me what happened next.

"Well, you could hear this woman's scream all throughout the store. But the story doesn't end there," he continued.

"There was a man and his son who heard the scream and came over to see what had happened. The woman pointed at me and said, 'He just fried me by reading my mind!' They were all as white as ghosts after that."

As this magic dealer told the story, I could see it all happening in my mind. The details were rich enough to help me picture it in my head. And when he said the woman screamed, I felt that rush of excitement that said, *"Get that trick, Joe!"*

And yes, I bought that trick.

And quite a few others.

This same dealer told me two more stories, about magic tricks he did for people and their reactions to them. In every case I was there, mentally, and I ended up buying the tricks.

If you haven't caught on yet, this is hypnotic selling at work.

I'm sure the magic dealer has no idea what hypnotic selling is. He doesn't know what the phrase Buying Trance means. He does this selling magic naturally. So let's review three key points to discover how he pulled off this "trick":

1. *He listened to me.*

    He couldn't offer any suggestions or stories to me until he first knew what I wanted. So he probed to discover that I wanted magic that made people gasp. That clued him to what he should offer me. Had I said I wanted magic for kids, I'm sure he would have told me a story about performing magic for children. He tailored his story to me. By doing so, he met me in my existing trance.

2. *He told true stories.*

He didn't make up his stories. He told me exactly what happened when he used these tricks in the real world. That subliminally communicated to me that he was honest and that these tricks would work for me, too. People are always making conclusions based on the little information you tell them. Always be honest, so trust is there when it's time for the order. Again, people buy only from people they know, like, and respect.

3. *He used lots of details.*

He told me what store he went to, the name of the woman he performed the trick for (I left them out of this chapter, though, to respect their privacy), and all the details of her reaction. This brought the story to life in my mind and made it easy for me to see myself performing and receiving the applause. People will generally live out in their heads the story you tell them. The more specifics you can offer, the easier it will be for them to relate to your story.

You get the idea. The Buying Trance is all about delivering a message to people that fits what *they* are looking for and that is delivered in a vivid way.

Do this and you'll see real magic. People will marvel at your storytelling skills—and they'll pay you real money, too.

And that's the best trick of all.

Note: The magic dealer was Emory Williams Jr. (www .williamsmagic.com).

The Most Important Chapter in This Entire Book

I don't blame you if you saw this chapter listed in the Table of Contents and then jumped to this page. Before you read too far past this sentence, though, stop and ask yourself *why* you skipped to this chapter.

My guess is that the title tickled your curiosity, which you've already learned is a powerful hypnotic trance inducer.

I would also guess that the title suggested that all you need to read is this single chapter to understand the entire concept of the Buying Trance, which means the title appealed to your desire for instant gratification.

Whatever your reasons for flipping by everything else to get to this chapter, it's worth reflecting and learning from. This behavior is exactly what your own clients and prospects are going through: They are preoccupied in their own little worlds (their trances) and they want you to get to the point. Meet them where they are already at, mentally, and you can guide them to where you want them to go.

That's how I got *you* here.

Now let me give you a detailed explanation of how I implement this process online, whenever I write sales letters, e-mails, web sites content, or blogs. As you can imagine, the online world is flooded with millions of web sites and the potential for distraction is enormous. Getting people to your web site or blog, and keeping them there, is the ultimate challenge.

I've found a way to succeed online using the Buying Trance. I've never revealed this system before, so you're in for a treat. Pull up a chair and let's get started.

THE SYSTEM

To simplify the explanation of how I put people into a Buying Trance online, I'll use my blog as an example. (If you want to see my blog, go to www.mrfire.com and look for the link to it on the left. Click it and you'll be there.)

Step 1: Choose your keyword.

The first thing I do when I want to write about something on my blog is make a mental note of the subject. For example, if I want to write about the cholesterol-lowering natural supplement I'm an investor in (see www.cardiosecret.com), I write down the keywords *cholesterol lowering*. If I want to write about the fitness program I'm in, I might use the keyword *fitness* or maybe *weight loss* as my focal point. If you're about to write about your accounting service, you might use *accounting* as your keyword. While the keyword is important, it's simply a starting point, so don't fret over it or what you think it needs to be. Take your best educated guess.

Step 2: Do a keyword search.

I then go to www.wordtracker.com and do a search for words similar to my selected keyword. This is important. Wordtracker is an online service that compiles a gigantic database of words being searched online. You enter some keywords (as in step 1) and Wordtracker tells you how often people search for them and, more importantly, offers words you may not have considered that people are searching for that tie in to what you want to write about. Wordtracker will also tell you how many other sites are using those same keywords, so you are aware of the competition. In short, Wordtracker generates a list of optimal keywords that you may want to consider using in your writing to grab more traffic from people searching for them.

Step 3: Use the new keywords in your blog.

I then write my blog post using as many of those new keywords as possible. In this way I am stuffing my blog entry with *known* search terms, all of which are *relevant* to my blog entry for that day.

What this three-step formula does is help me meet people where they are *mentally*. Again, to create a Buying Trance, I have to understand that people are preoccupied and I have to meet them *where they already are*. Wordtracker reveals the terms people are using to search online, which tells me what is on their minds. When I use those very terms, I am meeting people in their existing trances.

Let me walk you through an example so you understand this even more clearly.

MRFIREMELTDOWN.COM

As I write this, I just opened a brand-new site at www.mrfire meltdown.com. The goal of it is to sell a membership program where people receive a DVD every month revealing fitness and marketing secrets. I want to get people to the site, so they will subscribe to my DVD program. One way I will tell people about it is with a post on my blog. Here's how I might go about writing a post that ends up putting people into a Buying Trance.

First, I fire up www.wordtracker.com. I go into its "keyword universe" search function, which allows great flexibility in my detective work for the best keywords to use in my blog. I'll use *fitness marketing* as my key search phrase because the site I want to promote covers two very popular areas—fitness and marketing.

Wordtracker comes back with a long list of 300 related keywords. Here are the first 100 from the list it generated for me:

1. Fitness marketing
2. Fitness
3. Marketing
4. Martial arts software
5. EFT processing
6. Jobs
7. Marketing
8. Employment
9. Fitness
10. Nottingham
11. Health clubs
12. Fit
13. Martial arts schools marketing
14. ID cards
15. Third-party collections
16. Direct mail
17. Retention cards
18. Tournament insurance

19. Graphic design
20. Third-party Credit Card Processing
21. Lead boxes
22. Third-party billing
23. Retention tools
24. Accident insurance
25. Bodybuilding
26. Martial arts services
27. Credit reporting
28. Job
29. Martial arts school services
30. Membership cards
31. Postcards
32. Business
33. Computer software
34. Collections
35. ASF International
36. Billing
37. Health
38. Marketing tools
39. Financial services
40. Receivables management
41. Martial arts school management software
42. Electronic funds transfer
43. Credit card processing
44. Karate software
45. Claims services
46. General insurance
47. Check-in software

48. Third-party EFT processing
49. School management services
50. Modelling
51. Payment processing
52. Design
53. Personal trainer
54. Health club
55. Personal trainer marketing
56. In
57. Exercise
58. Marketing plan
59. Recruitment
60. Healthy
61. Personal training
62. Bodybuilders
63. Models
64. Sports
65. Resume
66. Odd jobs
67. Melbourne jobs
68. Dojang software
69. Finance and banking career in australia
70. Government jobs
71. Fitness business
72. Recruitment agencies
73. Jobs in Melbourne
74. Jobs online
75. Employment agencies
76. Job sites

77. Sydney jobs
78. Jobs in Sydney
79. Australian jobs
80. Adelaide jobs
81. Job search Australia
82. IT jobs
83. Employment Australia
84. Mycareer
85. MrMarketer
86. Mycareer.com.au
87. Career.com
88. One
89. B2B
90. Accounting jobs
91. B-to-B
92. Job search
93. Mycareer.com
94. My career
95. Fitness professionals
96. Jobs in Australia
97. Career
98. www.mycareer.com.au
99. One career
100. Brochures

Obviously, not every term on the list is relevant. What I do next is select the meaningful terms to find out how popular they are. Again, what I'm doing is hunting for the popular relevant terms my prospects are currently using. That helps reveal where their minds (trances) are at. In this case, just to give you an example of how this works, I'll select term 55, "personal trainer marketing," because I suspect personal trainers might be interested in a monthly DVD on marketing and fitness.

Wordtracker quickly comes back with 300 terms I might use. Here are the top five phrases:

1. Personal fitness trainers
2. Fitness personal trainers
3. Personal fitness trainers for teens
4. Marketing yourself as a personal trainer
5. Personal trainer marketing

Wordtracker lets me dig deeper ("Dig" function) if I want to see even more tangent words and phrases, all relevant to the ones I have. If I don't like what I see, I can always scrap them or just hit the back button on my computer and go back to the original list. In this case, I don't like the phrases and don't feel they are relevant to my www.mrfiremeltdown.com site, so I just go back to my original list and choose something else to search. In this case, I go back and select my original search term: *fitness marketing*. As a result, Wordtracker gives me this new list (partial):

Martial arts software

EFT processing

Health clubs

Fit

This list is a little more interesting, and I could work with it. But I want to go deeper. So I'll "dig" on the top phrase, "fitness marketing," to see what else surfaces. In this case, nothing else surfaces, so I'm left with my original term, "fitness marketing," as well as the others on the first list.

With these keywords in mind, I write my blog, weaving in

as many of the keyword search terms as possible. This is the easiest part of the formula. You simply write your blog and insert the phrases Wordtracker told you were relevant and popular. For example, I might write my blog as follows:

> My new site went live this morning at www.mrfiremeltdown .com. Anyone interested in fitness marketing should take a look at it. But I believe anyone wanting to know marketing for fitness centers or wanting a marketing plan for fitness centers or even people who want marketing software, especially personal train-ers, would want this new DVD of the month.

Obviously, this is not my best hypnotic writing. Nor would I leave it at that. It's my first draft. I wrote it in three seconds to show you how to embed Wordtracker's results into a piece of writing. I would not stop there in this process. I would take the formula to the following final step:

I then write the blog entry using every hypnotic writing trick in the book. I'd pull out a copy of my book, *Hypnotic Writing*, and brush up on the writing methods revealed in it. The end result might be something like this:

The Marketing and Fitness Secrets of a Melting Mr. Fire

Scott York came to my home gym yesterday and lit the torch un-der my feet. It was day one for our monthly DVD described at www.mrfiremeltdown.com.

He taught me his unusual 30-minute fitness routine—the one he used to lose 45 pounds.

He also spent time picking my brains about marketing.

I surprised him by some of the things I revealed about market-ing and publicity.

He surprised me by teaching me that I don't have to starve to lose weight quickly and easily.

This is gonna be one collectible, unusual, and unforgettable DVD!

My new site went live this morning at www.mrfiremeltdown .com. Anyone interested in fitness marketing should take a look at it. But I believe anyone wanting to know marketing for fitness centers or wanting a marketing plan for fitness centers or even people who want marketing software, especially personal trainers, would want this new DVD of the month.

I think you can call it Marketing with Muscle.

As you can see, this three-step formula helps you uncover the current trance people are in, so you are better equipped to write blog posts (or web sites or e-mails) that speak to their current interests. It's a proven way to create a Buying Trance online.

Finally, here's how the blog entry looked when it was finally posted:

Who Else Wants to Know the Marketing and Fitness Secrets of a Melting Mr. Fire?

Scott York came to my home gym yesterday (www.gladiatorgym.com) and lit the torch under my butt.

It was day one of filming for our monthly DVD described at www.mrfiremeltdown.com.

I was a nervous wreck before we began. I didn't know what to expect.

Would Scott be a Navy SEALS take-no-prisoners trainer?

Would he ask me countless marketing questions while I panted for air?

I'm relieved to say I survived it.

Scott taught me his unusual 30-minute fitness routine— the one he used to lose 45 pounds.

He also spent time picking my brains about marketing.

I surprised him by some of the things I revealed about marketing and publicity.

He surprised me by teaching me that I don't have to starve to lose weight quickly and easily. That was good news, as just the day before I was feeling light-headed from cutting back on my food and carbs. Scott pointed out that you don't need to suffer to lose weight and get fit.

And I pointed out that people can succeed with marketing if they do a few things consistently, like model the great showman, P.T. Barnum, who knew the value of publicity. (I wrote about Barnum in my book, *There's A Customer Born Every Minute*.)

This is gonna be one collectible, unusual, and unforgettable DVD.

The marketing-fitness site went live yesterday morning at www.mrfiremeltdown.com.

Anyone interested in fitness marketing should take a look at it.

But I believe anyone wanting to know marketing for fitness centers or wanting a marketing plan for fitness centers or even people who want marketing software, especially personal trainers, would want this new DVD of the month.

I think you can call it **Marketing with Muscle.**

Ao Akua,

Joe
www.mrfire.com

PS—Scott just e-mailed me one of the workouts he wants me to do. You'll get to see me do them on the monthly DVD. These are so intense that you may lose weight just *watching* me work out!

As you can see, using Wordtracker to help you incorporate the words and phrases people are currently searching for is a little-known way to begin to put people into a Buying Trance.

But let me confess something to you about this method: As a result of doing all of what I just explained to you, I learned that the site I wanted to promote at www.mrfiremeltdown.com wasn't working. It wasn't what people wanted. Even though I promoted it using every method I could think of, only one person signed up for the DVD I was trying to sell.

What went wrong? I obviously focused on me, and not on my prospects. While it seemed like a good idea at the time, by focusing on my own weight loss, I wasn't focusing on what the viewer would get. In short, I was breaking the Buying Trance state. As a result, I had to go back to the drawing board.

YOUR FITNESS BODY

My partner on this project, Scott York, and I talked over the problem and we decided that people might want a body and business contest. While there are numerous fitness contests available, run by actors such as Sylvester Stallone and companies such as EAS Inc., we had never heard of a body *and* *business* contest. The idea would have a contest where people worked on their fitness, as well as their business. Whoever showed the most transformation in both areas would win.

Scott and I decided to ask the market what they wanted. We didn't want to assume anything. Instead, we wanted to find out the current trance of people. So we sent out a survey. We asked if they wanted us to hold a fitness contest, a business contest, or a combination of both. To our surprise, the vast majority of people wanted a "double-whammy" contest. So that's what we called it. You can see it described at www.yourbusinessbody.com.

Was this new approach the ticket? Did this merge with the existing trance of people?

Apparently so. Within hours of our announcing it to a small list, dozens of people downloaded our rules and regulations. A few went and ordered the products we offered on the site, ranging from my recent book, *There's a Customer Born Every Minute*, to my best-selling Nightingale-Conant audio program, *The Power of Outrageous Marketing*, to the monthly DVD we wanted people to subscribe to.

The point of this confession is that you may have to test to find out what people want. Wordtracker and other tools can help you target your market. But you always have to focus on what people want, and not on what you want to sell, in order to create that Buying Trance.

Finally, let's end this chapter by showing you the e-mail we sent to explain our new positioning. You'll notice that this e-mail is focused on the reader, and it tells a story, which easily guides the reader into a Buying Trance. The letter is from my partner and trainer, Scott York.

> Dr. Joe Vitale's **YourBusinessBody.com**
> It's a Double–Whammy of a Challenge!

~~~~~~

Dr. Joe Vitale's $150,000 YourBusinessBody.com
Transformation Challenge!
This Is Exciting!
July 2006

~~~~~~

Greetings!

Big and exciting news!

Dr. Vitale and I were having a gut wrenching training session recently (well I was actually just training him) in Dr. Vitale's home gym.

He was sweating and I was filming.

I was filming for our fitness and marketing DVD of the month series for what started out as www.mrfiremeltdown.com.

It was another one of those **electrifying** training sessions where the creativity was thick, the business and **marketing ideas were enormous** - each better than the last.

As usual, the energy within those four walls of his home gym was huge!

I was training Dr. Vitale as well as asking him tons of questions about how to improve marketing, sales copy, create better websites, newsletters, etc.

At this point, I have studied most all of Dr. Vitale's work and so I wanted to know the answers to the questions that no one has asked him yet.

Sure, he got a little flustered at times.

Who wouldn't? Here he was grunting and groaning while someone was sticking a camera in his face asking him about marketing as well as having him do "**burpees**" at the same time!

Some of my fellow trainers out there reading this know exactly what I'm talking about and I can almost hear them chuckling.

 As you might already know, some of the best ideas come to you when you are engaging in physical activity.

Or soon after.

I left Dr. Vitale's gym that day, my head buzzing, with money-making ideas to last me 2 years!

My wife always makes fun of me when I get home because she says I have this "on top of the world" type of aura about me.

I'm a pretty positive guy to begin with but nothing takes the place of hanging around Dr. Vitale for a few hours every Saturday at his home gym.

He is a rarity. He is an absolute lightning rod for success and empowerment.

If this guy doesn't make you feel like you can unlock the treasure chest of success, fulfillment, and happiness then you may as well forget any sort of attempt at all.

I mean have you read *"The Attractor Factor"* or seen the movie "The Secret"?

As if it's not enough to see his BMW Z3, BMW 6 series, Nerissa's 2007 Toyota Camry Hybrid (these cars have a great new look) and his house, now he's talking about buying the actor James Caan's 2005 Bentley GT!

What does this guy know that you and I can benefit from?

While Dr. Vitale is one of the most down to earth and unassuming people that you will ever meet (he just happens to like cars), **he turns into a marketing monster** when we start filming this DVD of the month series.

I've learned **SO MUCH** since I've had the opportunity to train him, eat with him, hang out with him and really, really get to know him.

And so will you through these DVD's.

I will make sure of it.

So, OK so I'm getting close to the **big announcement**.

Upon my return from Dr. Vitale's home, my wife and I were discussing this project, www.mrfiremeltdown.com.

I said to her "You know, these DVD's are really going to be great and they are going to help so many people learn about marketing and fitness."

"But something is still missing."

I want this to be a crazy opportunity of a lifetime for as many people as we can reach.

Something that no one has done before.

We began talking about the Body for Life transformation challenge that Dr. Vitale is working towards.

My wife said "Why don't you make this a Body and Business Transformation Challenge?"

Eureka!

That was the missing ingredient.

That was the thing that will put this over the top and make it the most talked about event in the marketing world!

And one person is going to become the **GRAND CHAMPION!**

I emailed Joe and told him about my wife's idea (I wish I had thought of it :) and, of course, he loved it!

"Your wife is a genius!" he said.

For all of the details of this HUGE opportunity ($150,000.00 plus) rush on over to www.yourbusinessbody.com and read all of the details.

Check out the blog, the entry kit, round dates, the rules and then light a fire under your butt.

Because if this opportunity doesn't, what will?

Go to www.yourbusinessbody.com!

Best of Luck,

Scott (and Joe)

Contact Information

~~~~~~

email: mrfire@yourbusinessbody.com
phone: 512-233-0756
web: http://www.yourbusinessbody.com

~~~~~~

THE HYPNOTIC POWER OF AGREEMENT

Traditional sales and marketing often urge you to put people into a "yes" mind-set. The idea is to get prospects saying yes to a series of questions. The more you can get them to nod their head, the better the odds of your making a sale when you ask them to buy.

The "yes" method is a hypnotic technique. But hypnotists do it with *agreement*. Although leading people to say yes is a smart move, a simpler, wiser, and more effective approach is to get into agreement with them.

At the basic level, this means never arguing with them, never countering their objections, and never making them wrong. As I wrote in my book, *Life's Missing Instruction Manual*, you can avoid arguments and win friends simply by never making someone wrong. Instead, agree with them. You can always find something to agree on. When you do, you create this hypnotic state of agreement.

Here's an example of how this works.

NERISSA'S NEW CAR

I bought my love a new car. She wanted a hybrid, which saves gas by running on batteries part of the time. It had to be special-ordered. We looked in the brochures and decided on the 2007 Toyota Camry hybrid. We picked the options and color she wanted. We were told it would take seven weeks to build overseas and then ship to us in the States. We placed the order and made a deposit. After only a few weeks, the car arrived. We went to see it last night.

Nerissa's first impression was not good.

She didn't like the car.

Here are a few reasons why:

- The car was parked under a red tent. That made the silver-colored car look pink.

- The trunk in the car was very small, due to the huge batteries back there.

- The car's style didn't match what we saw in the brochure.

- The car seemed smaller on the inside than what we expected.

I wasn't about to argue with Nerissa about the car. It's her car. It's her choice to get what she loves. Besides, I didn't have any investment in buying that particular car. I wouldn't make any money buying it. In fact, since I was the one buying it as a gift for her, I would be out a lot of money. So I kept my mouth shut and simply supported Nerissa. But by now, she had tears in her eyes. She was disappointed.

I wondered how the salesman would handle this situation. Traditional car salespeople can be pushy. Since this gentleman was going to make a lot of money off of a cash sale, rather than the lesser money he would make off a financed sale, I knew he wouldn't like Nerissa's disappointment. He didn't want to lose the sale.

When the salesman returned, I told him, "We have a snag."

I looked into his face and saw his eyes squint and his breathing change. He was bracing himself for bad news.

"She doesn't like the car," I told him. I then told him why. I went on to say, "We'd like to take some pictures of the car and go home and think about it. We'll let you know tomorrow if we decide to buy it or not."

The salesman nodded and said, "Okay, that sounds good." He then added, "What if you could take the car home for the night?"

I thought that was brilliant, but Nerissa didn't want the obligation of having the car on her hands, or the pressure of caring for something she might decide she doesn't want. She suggested we just go take more pictures of the car and talk about it. The salesman agreed and let us go out to the car.

I have no idea if the salesman beat his head against the wall after we left his office, or if he cursed us in his mind or under his breath, but he never disagreed with us. His agreement to something he clearly did not want was letting this situation evolve in a more relaxed way.

Nerissa and I spent some time sitting with the car and talking. I didn't argue with any of her feelings. I let her express her concerns and process her thoughts. I let her know I was fine if she wanted the car, and fine if she didn't.

As we talked, I noticed her face relax. She went from having tears in her eyes to a light in them. She went from a flushed face to a radiant face. She went from a tense forehead to a smooth one. By the time we went back inside the dealership, she had decided to buy the car. We did, too. It's in our garage as I write these words.

CREATING AGREEMENT WITHOUT WORDS

The point here is that arguing with people puts them into a fight or flight trance. That's not a Buying Trance. In order to lead people into the trance you want them to go in, you need to agree with them—no matter where they are when they come to you. One way to create this agreement, without saying a word, is demonstrated in the following story:

One night not long ago I watched a documentary on Milton Erickson. I noticed that he smiled a lot. Whenever someone came to him for therapy, he met them with this disarming big smile and beaming, happy eyes. Although I never met Erickson, whenever I think of his smile in that film, I smile. I instantly like the man. I can imagine how easily he put his clients into trance states because his smile helped them relax. His smile helped them trust him.

I remember a client from years ago who said she kept a mirror by her phone. Whenever she made a call or received a call, she looked in the mirror and smiled. She knew that her smile would change her voice. Even when her listener couldn't see her, they could feel the smile.

A great way to induce a trance is to smile.

Why not smile right now?

DON'T READ
THIS CHAPTER

M any so-called communication experts keep declaring that your mind cannot process a negative command. They say that "Don't spill the milk" means you'll spill the milk. They say your mind doesn't respond to "don't" and in fact skips over it. As a result, you end up seeing the rest of the statement as a command. You then spill the milk.

I disagree. The very first words most children hear are "No" and "Don't." We learn right away not to poop in our pants, or eat the dirt, or swing the cat by the tail, or spill our milk. The only reason we might still spill our milk is sheer awkwardness or clumsiness, not because of a communication issue.

This is one of the things wrong with neuro-linguistic programming (NLP) and other communication modalities that claim to know how our brains work. They make wild claims and act as if they are universal truths. Yet the truth is, no one really knows how the brain works. We're still learning. To say

we don't process negative commands is an arrogant statement. It assumes godlike powers. And it's wrong.

Look at the title of this chapter. I inserted the word *don't*.
Why? Because the word actually helps make the title more interesting. It increases persuasion. Had I said, "Read This Article," you might *not* read it simply because it seemed
uninteresting. But I added "Don't," and suddenly you're curious. "Why doesn't Joe want me to read this?" you wonder.
"Don't" was seen and registered by your mind. You didn't
miss it, did you?

Again, communication is more than assumptions about
how our minds process information. You learned what many
negative words meant before you were three years old. Your
unconscious mind is well aware of what they mean today.

Don't tell others about this book.

Don't pass this book to your coworkers or employees.

Don't go buy all my books and tapes.

Don't send me money.

You see the word *don't* and you'll do what you please. If
you want to pass this book to friends, you will. If you don't,
you won't. My trying to trick you with a negative command
is ridiculous. You're smarter than that, aren't you?

Kevin Hogan, the author of *The Psychology of Persuasion*,
says, "Negative command words in general indicate the person will remember or code in deeper whatever was discussed. This doesn't mean they will act one way or the other.
It simply makes the command/idea/request more likely to
be remembered."

Exactly. My adding "Don't" to the title of this chapter simply made it more memorable. It didn't *make* you read this section at all.

The only time the "don't" trick works is to get someone to
think of something. In other words, if I say, "Don't think of
Sophia Loren," you can't help but think of the famous actress.

But thinking is different from action. Yes, thinking can *lead* to action. But what we're focusing on here is communication.

If I say, "Don't think of buying my books," you will think of buying them, at least for a second.

But if I say, "Don't buy my books," it does not mean you will run out and buy them. You are not a robot.

Careful use of negative commands is important when weaving a Buying Trance. If you tell someone a negative, thinking they will do the opposite of what you say, you may break rapport and awaken the person.

For example, if you say, "Don't buy this new car right now," you may shake the person's trance because of the awkward statement. But if you say, "Don't buy this car until I've answered all of your questions," you may be closer to what the person wants to hear. You'll also be planting a presumptuous phrase that can lead to the sale. In other words, you are saying, "Once I answer all of your questions, you will buy this new car."

Let's wake up. Let's realize that we are smarter than generalized rules of language. Let's stop pretending we are all trained monkeys.

Don't you agree?

LISTEN TO THIS: HOW TO CREATE BUYING TRANCES FOR RADIO

W hat about running commercials on radio?
How do you write them so they create a Buying Trance in the people listening?

With so many stations playing everything from jazz to rap and broadcasting political debates as well as weather reports, how do you create a radio spot that gets heard?

I was once very resistant to running ads on the radio. Since I come from the direct marketing school, which likes measurable results, radio seemed like throwing money at birds. You pay your money, record the ads, hear them broadcast on the air—and then they're gone. It seemed pointless to me.

I knew you could create a two-step ad, of course. That's where you record and broadcast a radio spot that people hear, which directs them to call a number or visit a web site.

There's nothing wrong with a two-step radio ad. But again, how do you record one that people not only pay attention to, but stop and act on?

LISTEN TO WENDI

One day I heard a radio commercial from Wendi Friesen. Wendi runs the Internet's largest hypnosis resource center. She started her company with nothing, when she was broke and desperate. Today her online business at www.wendi.com has millions of dollars of revenue a year. She has 17 employees and can hardly keep up with all the business. One of Wendi's marketing secrets is her radio spots. She spends $1 million a year to air her commercials. Apparently they work.

When I first heard a spot by Wendi, I was struck by how it charmed me into listening to her. There were no bells and whistles. No jingles. No music, stupid dialogue, jokes, or anything else to distract me from her message. It was Wendi talking directly to me—at least that's how it felt. As a result, I never forgot her, her voice, or her web site. I've been a regular customer of her site ever since.

But that's not all that happened.

ATTRACTING SUCCESS

As a result of hearing Wendi's hypnotic ads, I decided to run some of my own. When I was preparing my national marketing strategy to promote my recent book, *The Attractor Factor*, I budgeted a few thousand dollars for a week's worth of radio spots on satellite radio. I then went into the recording studio and recorded a few commercials.

I modeled what Wendi had done: I spoke right to the listener. In the same way that I write my books or sales letters or web sites, I pretended it was just you and me. This personal style created a captivating hypnotic trance. While the words can't convey the power of the audio, here are a couple of the scripts I used:

Let me ask you a question: What are you attracting into your life? I've learned that most of the self-help books and tapes out there are missing a secret step—a step that you must have in order to achieve the goals you say you want. If you don't do this missing step, you are not likely to get the result you say you want. You'll go on diets and fall off of them and wonder why. You'll try to get more money and always fall short. You'll try to get healthy or find the perfect love, but keep hitting a block. What's happening? Your inner state of mind, the one that is your primary operating system, is not in alignment with your conscious intent. I'm Joe Vitale and I have a solution. It will all be revealed on April 5th. For now, go see www.attractorfactor.com. Remember, you *can* have what you want—once you know the secret. See www.attractorfactor.com.

Are you having trouble achieving your goals? Maybe you want to lose weight but keep falling off your diet. Maybe you are trying really hard to get healthy, or earn more money, or find the perfect love, but something keeps stopping you. I'm here to tell you it's not your fault! It *is* your responsibility. You simply need to know the five-step formula for getting clear so you can have, do, or be whatever you want. I know you are skeptical. But thousands have already proven that this system works. I'll reveal it all on April 5th. For now, go see www.attractorfactor.com.

Did the radio ads work?

The Attractor Factor became a #1 best seller online at Amazon. It also knocked out of first place the latest Harry Potter book, which no other author or book had done for the *previous six months*. In short, the results were staggering.

When you consider recording your own radio spots, keep in mind what I learned from Wendi:

- Speak to your listeners as if you are sitting across from them. This means using a conversational voice. You wouldn't yell, scream, sing, or throw a fit to get the attention of a prospect if you were standing in their office. You'd be yourself. Be yourself on radio, too.

- Address what is on their minds, not yours. If you know your target audience (and you should), then you have a good sense of where they are mentally when your commercial airs. Maybe they are working. Or they may be driving. If so, you might begin your spot with words that tie in to what your listeners are doing: "If you're driving around the city right now, wondering where you'll eat for lunch, then let me tell you about this. . . ."

- Tell them to do something. All ads need a call to action. Tell your listeners what you want them to do. Wendi asked people to visit her web site at www.wendi.com. I asked people to see my web site at www.attractorfactor.com. Always end with a direction.

As you can see, radio—or any audio media, such as podcasts—can be a vehicle for a Buying Trance.

But what about television and other video?

Watch This: How to Create Buying Trances for Television or Video

O ne of the television commercials that I see almost every night begins with the words, "Home owners . . ." The ad rarely changes. One time I noticed there was a different spokesperson. But clearly the person speaking isn't as important as what he or she says.

Why does the ad begin with the words "Home owners"?

By now you should know that that phrase is speaking directly to the people the ad is designed to reach. It is meeting them in their current trance state. Only home owners will be interested in the ad. Only home owners should listen to the ad, because the commercial is designed to sell refinancing of the homes of current owners. By calling out the home owners, the ad is speaking the personal name of each viewer.

Let me put it this way: If your name is Mary and the television commercial begins with, "Hi, Mary," you would sit up and take notice. Or if your name is Tony and the ad begins, "Hello there, Tony," you would pay attention—at least long enough to understand whether the message is really for you.

The same thing is happening with every television or videotaped piece. The opening of it needs to merge with the current mentality of the person watching it. If it doesn't, there won't be a Buying Trance.

How do you create a Buying Trance in the visual world? Let's see.

TELEVISED TRANCES

If you keep in mind everything you've learned in this book so far, creating a Buying Trance for any medium ought to be a snap. For example:

Roy Garn taught us that people have four basic preoccupations: self-preservation, romance, money, and recognition. If you take any one of them, you can use it to lead people into a Buying Trance. If you want to address the money element, you might begin your commercial or video with a focus on money: "Are you looking for ways to save more money?" As simple as that question is, it works because the vast majority of people are interested in the subject.

By the same token, if you wanted to focus on the recognition strategy, you might begin your spot with something like, "You could win a trip to Maui by entering the world's first body and business contest at www.yourbusinessbody.com." With this approach you suggest the reward of standing out from the crowd: recognition.

You can take any of Roy Garn's insights or Elmer

Wheeler's points, and turn them into Buying Trances in the visual world.

But you don't have to stop there.

DOG-GONE GOOD FUN

In one of my earlier books, *The Seven Lost Secrets of Success*, I explained that people will spend their last nickel to have fun. What they are doing is seeking relief, or escape, from the boredom of their lives. Henry David Thoreau was right when he said the average person led a life of quiet desperation. As a result, people seek out fun.

In 2006 I held a publicity stunt called the Canine Concert. It was an event where a band pretended to play music at a sound level only dogs could hear. The stunt was a hoax to bring attention to my book on P. T. Barnum, titled *There's a Customer Born Every Minute*.

We videotaped the entire event, of course. There were magicians Kent Cummins and John Maverick; a living mermaid and a fake mermaid; the local Austin, Texas, band called Porter Davis; and more. It was a lively event on a hot day in Texas. (You can see clips and pictures at www.canineconcert.com.)

When Nerissa Oden edited the footage from the event to make a DVD I would sell later, she made sure she added upbeat music, humorous clips from interviews, shots of dogs, and even one shot of a protesting cat. Why? All of this was designed to *hold people's attention*. The longer we can hold attention, the longer they stay in the Buying Trance.

What did the DVD sell? Why did we want people to stay focused on what they were watching?

Again, the event as well as the DVD were set up to bring attention to my book on P. T. Barnum. What I obviously wanted them to buy was the book.

THE SECRET

The key in creating Buying Trances in any visual medium is the same as in creating a Buying Trance anywhere else—focus on the prospect, not on you.

Why does this hold true in every medium? The answer is in the book *What Happy Companies Know: How the New Science of Happiness Can Change Your Company for the Better*, by Nan Baker, Cathy Greenberg, and Collins Hemingway:

> Humans went from the first powered airplane ride to a safe round trip to the moon in 66 years, yet written and archeological records show that human behavior, good and bad, both cultured and cruel, is largely unchanged over at least the span of our written history and possibly much longer.

While technology may change, people don't. Appeal to their interests—no matter what media you do it in—and you will begin to put them into a Buying Trance.

A SECRET BUYING TRANCE INDUCTION

There are several advanced methods of leading someone into a Buying Trance. I wrote about a few of them in my earlier book, *Hypnotic Writing*. In this chapter I want to reveal an advanced covert method of leading people from where they are mentally to where you want them to be: buying your goods.

I went to copywriter Harlan Kilstein and asked him for his most record-breaking sales letter. Harlan is the author of *Steal This Book! Million Dollar Sales Letters You Can Legally Steal to Suck in Cash like a Vacuum on Steroids*. He's a persuasion expert first and a copywriter second. As a result, he thinks in terms of language and persuasion before he thinks in terms of writing copy. I've seen many sales letters by him. More often than not, they make me buy his product. That's a good sign. I'm not an easy mark. With that in mind, I wanted to know his secrets for putting people into a Buying Trance. Before I tell you what those secrets are, read the letter he sent me. that he wrote for Sylvia. Here it is:

Dear Spiritual Seeker:

On a beautiful late spring afternoon, twenty-five years ago, two young women graduated from the same high school. They were very much alike, these two young women. Both had been better than average students, both were likeable and both—as young women are—were filled with ambitious dreams for the future.

Recently, these women returned to their high school for their 25th reunion.

They were still very much alike. Both were happily married. Both had beautiful children. And both, it turned out, had similar careers and even lived in their old neighborhood.

But there was a difference. One of the women felt alone and unloved. The other had every single one of her heart's desires.

What Made The Difference?

Have you ever wondered, as have I, what makes such a dramatic difference in people's lives? It isn't always money or talent or hard work. It isn't that one person wants success and the other doesn't.

The difference lies in how attuned each person is to the spiritual forces around them and how they can tap into that power to have a more abundant life.

The difference lies in how you open yourself up to your personal angels and spirit guides and allow them to bless your life.

And that is why I am writing to you today during this holiday season. While most people are busy shopping and getting caught up in all the excitement, the real purpose of this period is getting connected to the powers of the universe. Discovering the ability to tap into the source of ultimate power, meaning, happiness, love and fulfillment.

My Wish For You For The Holiday Season

You see, people like Montel and Larry King often ask me, "Sylvia, what do you really want out of life?" And I always answer the same way.

My life's dream is that you be as open as I am to the Spiritual world around us. That you become in touch with your guides and that you learn to trust them to lead you to the magical life that awaits your call.

Each day, people like you attain their fondest dreams, true love, health, and abundance when you need it most.

And today I am really excited because you can help my dream come true as you open up the door to a new life.

An Opportunity For You Unlike Any Other

Right now my fondest dream for you is to let me take you by the hand and personally guide you through the spiritual maze to the pot of gold on the other side.

What's in your pot of gold? Is it true love? Is it health? Is it wealth and abundance? Is it a more spirit filled life?

My personal promise to you is that I am going to give you the opportunity to open your eyes and your heart to the other world—to the world where all your dreams become real.

I have created a special course for you. I call it God, Creation and Tools for Life. My teachings have three voices. Of course my own is present, but I also have two communicating spirit guides, Francine and Raheim, who are the major contributors. Francine's voice is audible to me but, as you know, relaying her information orally is not the most efficient form of communication. By special arrangement with God, I am able to allow Francine and Raheim to take control of my body so that they can communicate directly with you.

Only You Can Make My Dreams For You Come True

Think of your deepest desire right now. The one that only you and your angels know about. You know the one. We're about to set out on a journey to fulfill that dream.

In your unique course, I have given over hundreds of hours of spiritual energy to be your guide, your teacher, and your confidant. Through state-of-the-art technology, we will talk and you will share your feelings. My meditations will guide you to that special place where all your dreams come true.

With your permission, I would like to share the closing of a prayer that I begin this course with: "We will truly be a light in a lonely desert that enlightens many."

Would you like to be that light to shine on the lives of those around you as I have? Remember those two women that I talked about at the beginning of this letter. Their lives were so similar and yet so different. One was lonely and one was abundant.

What made their lives different? The ability to sense the richness of the Divine in all creation. Come with me now on this journey.

Click here to join me on this journey

A Life of Promise Awaits You – Now

This course has taken all of my energies. It is filled with special audio meditations that will speak to you on your computer. Each time you listen to them, I transfer some of that psychic energy to you.

I have included some of my very favorite video clips. We will explore fear and betrayal, illness and loneliness. And finally, we will graduate together to soul mates and love.

You see, I would not be a very good teacher if I didn't prepare you for the different times of your life now, would I?

My life's gift to you is the opportunity to join me in this course.

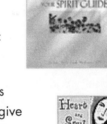

Francine has a gift for you as well. She wants you to have my new book, *Contacting Your Spirit Guide*. In it is a beautiful CD with a meditation on contacting your spirit guide. Francine wants you to succeed at every step of the way on our journey together.

Finally, Raheim has a gift for you too. He wants to be part of your life as well and he wants to give you a beautifully illustrated Heart and Soul card deck. And I want you to know something - a deep secret. If you prepare your heart and choose a card, your own spirit guide will provide your answer.

Click here to join me on this journey

How You Can Invite Blessing into Your Life

Right now, my accountants and bookkeeper won't talk to me. When they heard what I wanted to do they were very upset. But then I told them how special you are to me. So they finally agreed. (It was really the angels at work but don't tell them!) So the deal is on for just a short while.

For just 15 cents a day, you can have the spirit filled life of your dreams. That's all it takes. Your life with be enriched. Your prayers will be answered.

Of course, if you called me by phone, it would cost $700 an hour (when I'm available and there's usually a waiting list).

But, until December 25, I am going to let you have our gifts for you this season for just $59. That's what has my accountants so upset.

You see, each of the elements in the package is worth so much more spiritually.

But you really are going to have to act quickly before they make me withdraw this offer.

Right now, I want you to listen to the voice inside your heart that is telling you to do this.

If you hear the call, order it now. If you only hear the whisper of the angels' wings on the breeze outside, you really need this to open yourself up to the abundant love that awaits you.

Which of those two women do you want to be, lonely or abundant?

<u>Click here to join me on this journey</u>

The Conscious Guarantee: We are willing to take ALL the risk of your participation in this system. Take the Tools for Life course and follow the simple steps, the exercises, and the action plan we have put together for you. If for any reason you feel this course does not deliver much more than the value you paid for it, then simply let us know within 90 days and return the book/CD set and the cards and we will refund your money, no questions asked.

The only reason we can make such an ironclad, 100% money back guarantee is because we know that the information you are about to receive will help you impact your life.

Love, Light and Abundant Blessings

Sylvia Browne

PS. You know I have never made an offer like this before. I'm so excited that you are going to join me. Remember, I'm taking all the risk here and your new more spiritual life is guaranteed.

PPS. Here's the funny part. My accountants and bookkeeper just joined in the Holiday spirit. They want to give you a special gift as well. It's a beautiful screensaver for your computer.

<u>Click here to join me on this journey</u>

THE SECRET: NESTED LOOPS

Now here is Harlan's explanation for the success of his letter:

This letter was the first sales letter I wrote for the company, Conscious One. They were just getting started on the Internet and were not familiar with long-copy direct-sales letters. In the past they had only used HTML postcards.

They had a holiday-themed e-mail that needed to go out and they had a 36-hour deadline. I had never heard of Sylvia Browne (note: a best-selling author of New Age books) and hit the ground running.

Most copywriters will recognize this letter as an imitation of the famous Martin Conroy "*Wall Street Journal* Letter," which was one of the most successful direct-mail letters of all time. In fact, the *WSJ* letter was itself a swipe of a much earlier letter that I've traced as far back as the late nineteenth century!

And here, I adapted a little bit of the tone of that *WSJ* letter as well as the goal of moving readers in the direction of spirituality.

The *WSJ* letter was written to men and this letter was written to women so the language reflects the effort of writing to the female audience. My training as a copywriter began with my studies of neuro-linguistic programming (NLP). Many people have written about NLP as applied to writing, but they are generally referring to extremely manipulative embedded commands such as "Of course, you want to order right now, don't you?" That's the kind of use of NLP that gives it a bad name.

I'm all for the elegant use of NLP, and let me introduce you to one of the concepts used in this letter: It's called *nested loops*.

This methodology comes from the work of famed psychiatrist Milton Erickson, who used a technique of embedding stories within one another.

Here is a sample structure of nested loops:

Begin story A.

Begin story B.

Begin story C.

Begin story D.

Give instructions.

End story D.

End story C.

End story B.

End story A.

The use of this technique masks the fact that you are giving instructions. If you leave some of the loops open, you can create amnesia and people will forget the instructions you want them to follow.

So you need to close your loops. As you read the Sylvia Browne letter, pay attention to the loops as I open and close them. (Of course, none of this is in the original *WSJ* letter.)

One of the things I've done in this letter is introduce controversy. If you'll go through the letter to "How You Can Invite Blessing into Your Life," you'll see the section about "my accountants and bookkeeper won't talk to me" and how they don't think that this deal is too good and, therefore, it's a very limited deal.

Now, the idea of controversy is disturbing to a lot of people and, therefore, go down to the PPS of the letter and you see that the accountants and the bookkeeper join in the holiday spirit and they give you a gift as well.

If you do not resolve that controversy, if you do not resolve the argument, there is an open loop in the person's mind and, as those who have studied NLP know, opening loops but not closing them creates a risk of amnesia and that people are going to forget exactly what you wanted them to do, which in this case was to order.

Now a little bit of a technical problem was that this letter did very well and Conscious One heard from the Hay House publishers that they didn't want the letter going out with Sylvia Browne's name on it. So the first thing that we did was change the signature to a female staff member at Conscious One. Today it goes out with the name of Scott Martineau on it. Scott is the president of Conscious One. The change in signature has not had any impact on sales.

—Harlan Kilstein, EdD (www.overnight-copy.com)

THE PSYCHIC DEMAND EXAMPLE

After reading Harlan Kilstein's example and his explanation, I decided to quickly write a sales letter using his nested loops theory. Here's the letter. See if you can spot the nested loop.

"I Demand $25,000.00"

Just discovered — The 1910 Secret of *Psychic Demand*—The Long Lost Method for Getting What You Want — Guaranteed to *Always* Work!

Introducing a rare volume in a lost scientific course on success.

This is the actual secret method used by Joseph, Abraham, Moses, Plato, Phidias, Shakespeare and other legends throughout history.

Read this incredible true story and discover the secret that
commands the universe . . . a secret you will be able to use, too . . .
in only minutes from right now . . .

Dear Friend,

"I Demand $25,000.00"

That's what a sign in a beautiful gold frame read above the desk of
an executive's office in the early 1900's.

Many people looked at it. Some laughed. Some were curious. But
few knew what it meant.

Years later the same executive replaced the old gold framed sign
with a new one. This one read —

"I Demand $100,000.00"

Again, he left the sign on the wall above his desk. He rarely if ever
explained why it was there. Few people asked about it, oblivious to
what was actually happening.

And then again, years later, a new gold framed sign went above his
desk. This one read —

"I Demand $1,000,000.00"

What was the purpose of the signs?

Why were they in gold frames?

Why did they keep increasing in amounts?

You have to remember all of this was happening before 1910. Even
today, in 2006, those sums of money are impressive.

But to be demanding $25,000, or $100,000 or *one million dollars*
— in 1910?

That's either ludicrous or . . . miraculous.

I recently discovered a little booklet that explains what those
signs were doing and the science behind them.

I found the booklet and the story behind them rather . . . hypnotic.

Let me tell you about it...

The Amazing Story Behind "Mastery of Success"

The booklet was by Frank Channing Haddock. You may or may not know his name. He's famous for a book titled *Power of Will*.

But few know he wrote a series of 30 little books, consisting of 60 lessons, called *Mastery of Success*. They're rare to find in the original set. And very expensive if you do manage to unearth a complete set.

One of my readers found an incomplete set of the books one day and offered them to me. While she loves my work, she didn't just hand the books over to me. I had to pay a hefty fee to own them. But I gladly did. The books are worth gold.

When the big box of books arrived, I went to a private area and opened them. I was in a hypnotic state of focused attention as I carefully flipped through the old, dusty, brittle volumes.

Every book seemed like it contained a magic spell for getting what I wanted . . . whether love, money, sex, power, recognition, health, happiness, or . . . you name it.

But one of the books jumped out at me as being THE book to get, to own, to read, to learn and practice.

This one book alone began with a hook that wouldn't let me go.

I still can't believe how incredible it is . . .

Introducing "Psychic Demand"

It was a later volume from the set, about "Psychic Demand."

The name had a nice ring to it, and made me want to learn more.

As I read, I became more fascinated. You might say it was a 1910 version of my book, *The Attractor Factor*, which is all about the power of intention.

But Psychic Demand is even more powerful.

With Psychic Demand, you essentially *will* the universe to give you what you want.

This is huge.

In fact, I worry that this magic formula could get into the wrong hands.

Pat O'Bryan and I decided that we would use Psychic Demand to only attract ethical people to this site. That's why we will not advertise this site, or do anything to bring the riff-raff here.

We are attracting only ethical people — people who care about their family, friends, and the planet.

I'm hoping that person is you.

In fact, that's why you're here.

You're ready for this secret . . .

Psychic Demand Gives You Alexander-the-Great Power to Rule Your Life

With Psychic Demand, you can indeed will the universe to give you what you want.

But if you come from ego, you may will things to yourself that will cause you to hurt yourself. You have to be intelligent enough, and evolved enough, to balance what you want with what the universe wants for you. When you come from that inner place of power, Psychic Demand can be the "open sesame" to a glorious world of riches.

Yes, Psychic Demand is about using your will to influence the world.

But this is not a magic wand.

This is nuclear power.

This is not a Harry Potter trick.

This is a Merlin-like way to become Alexander the Great over your own life.

As you can imagine, this is not child's play.

Are you really ready for this kind of power?

Here's the story—

Here's what you will get when you order "Psychic Demand: the Course" today:

Psychic Demand: The Secret Lost Volume. The original booklet was written in 1910 by Haddock. We scanned it and you will get the exact copy of the original, as a PDF. This contains the entire "Psychic Demand" formula. Nothing is left out.

Bonus: And if you order today, you can also have a copy of the rare booklet, **At Your Command**, by Neville. This book was about Psychic Demand, but in terms of the 1930s. This is one of my favorite books. You will get the entire original book as a PDF.

All in all, this is a package to awaken your powers of manifestation—to help you have, do, or be whatever you want.

And the price for it all is only $19.

Yes, this package is guaranteed.

But what we guarantee is that we will deliver the goods promised. We do not guarantee your results because it is up to YOU to apply the Psychic Demand method. You can't buy a hammer and return it when you don't use it, saying "It doesn't work." Of course it works.

If you use this method, it will work. But if you're not happy, Clickbank (the company who handles the orders) will replace any defective item within 8 weeks, as they see fit.

Again, we don't want just anyone to have this.

For the sake of all concerned, do not order right now if you will use this to try to manipulate others or to do harm in the world. We only want advanced souls to use this power—and to use it for good.

You can order it right here (www.PsychicDemand.com).

About those Gold Framed "Demands" . . .

In case you are still curious, the executive who kept hanging gold framed "demands" above his desk went on to become a millionaire—around 1910.

One of the reasons his use of Psychic Demand worked is explained in the book you can order and have today, when Haddock says:

"Your ability to influence matter and mind in the present guarantees power over the so-called future, since the future is but the logical sequence of the present."

Statements like that one are what I love about Haddock's work. He is reminding you that you have more power than you ever imagined before. And all you need to do to begin using this power right now is to take action in this moment.

As he would explain, what you do *right now* will create what happens to you in the "future."

Psychic Demand can bring peace and plenty to the world we share.

It can bring health, happiness, wealth—or anything else you want.

Please use it for good.

Expect Miracles,

Dr. Joe Vitale
www.mrfire.com

PS — What will you demand for yourself once you learn the Psychic Demand method? Remember, Psychic Demand is extremely powerful. If you feel drawn to this rare material and proven method, then order it right now. You can have it in only minutes. But if you are skeptical or doubting or unsure, then please forget about this and move on. Or if what you want to do with this power is to control others or to overindulge in your own desires, then please don't order. We wish you all good things. We love you. All is well. May the light be with you.

EXPLANATION

My sales letter was quickly written, so don't judge it too harshly. There are many essentials missing from it (such as testimonials), but note the main reason for the letter: the nested loop.

I began the letter with a story. As you know by now, stories are hypnotic. They are a proven way to capture and hold attention. This particular story has built-in charm, as the tale of the gold frames makes people interested.

But also notice that I do not complete the story at first. What I do is begin the story, which is the loop opening. I then talk about the book I discovered, and the value of it. I keep going with that theme, right down to asking people to order the book.

It's only *after* I've asked the reader to click and order that I begin to close the loop to the opening story. In other words, I began the letter with a story, along the way stopped telling the story and asked people to buy my product, and then went back and completed the story. The completion is under the subhead "About Those Gold-Framed 'Demands.'"

Again, this is all an example of an advanced writing method to lead people into a Buying Trance. I urge you to practice this one. It's powerful, and can certainly increase your sales. In fact, let me prove it to you.

I put the sales letter I quickly wrote online, at www. psychicdemand.com. I told my list about the site with this brief e-mail:

Subject: A discovery of demand

I just found a technique that's far more powerful than the power of intention.

In fact, intention is for wimps.

I wish I had known this new method when I wrote my book, *The Attractor Factor.*

At least I know it now. You can, too.

Go see—

www.psychicdemand.com.

You'll love it.

Joe

As a result, sales happened virtually instantly. Within *seconds* there were five orders. Within 30 minutes there were over $1,000 in orders. Within one hour there were $3,000 in orders. Within 24 hours there were $10,000 in sales. And keep in mind these sales were for a $19 product.

It should be obvious: Nested loops are a proven way to help lead people into a Buying Trance.

YOUR GRANDFATHER WAS RIGHT

Two friends dropped by yesterday. We were talking business and I told them about the nested loops theory. I spontaneously began to explain it like this:

"It's a lot like how your grandfather might talk," I began. "Some old-timers inadvertently use nested loops when they start talking. They begin to tell you a story about being in World War II, but they don't finish it. Instead, they then start to tell you about their mother's cooking and the special Thanksgiving holiday they had one year, but they don't finish that, either. They then go on and tell you what they did that morning, when they went to get the newspaper off the front lawn.

"Most grandfathers who tell stories like this often forget to finish them," I explain. "But imagine right when old grand-dad stops telling you about this morning, he suddenly asks you to do him a favor. Since he's your grandfather, you'll probably comply.

"But even if you don't do him the favor right away, he goes on to finish the story about this morning, and then finish the story about Thanksgiving, and then finish the story about World War II.

"What he just did was weave a set of nested loops, insert-ing a request in the middle of it before closing the loops."

That's how nested loops work.

Or, as Milton Erickson is reported to have said, according to *The Wisdom of Milton H. Erickson* by Ronald Havens, "I also sometimes tell irrelevant stories and make non sequitur re-marks to induce confusion."

Confusion, as it turns out, is a very useful Buying Trance. So, if you're confused right now, it's a good thing.

THE SURPRISE GIFTS: A REVEALING SUMMARY

This morning I received a mysterious package by FedEx. It was a large white box marked "Perishable" in orange letters. There wasn't any note or return address. It was apparently a gift from a well-meaning stranger.

I carefully opened the box, not knowing if I'd find a live lobster or a bomb. I had to dig through some loose packaging materials and two large, frozen packets designed to keep the contents chilled. After digging even deeper, I found a package of some strange-looking meat. The label said it was chitterlings.

While I live in Texas and maybe chitterlings are popular here, I had no idea what they were. I had to Google them to learn they are pork intestines. Pork guts would not have been on my request list. Still, I know whoever sent the gift did it from a good intention. The point is, it was not appropriate for me. It broke any chance for a connection, let alone a Buying Trance.

Contrast that with a gift I received another time. A fellow coming out with a new course on persuasion wanted to get my attention. He did his homework and learned I love the music of Stevie Ray Vaughan. He hunted around and found a rare CD of Stevie's music. He sent the gift to me, along with his package. I have never forgotten him or his gift. His gift matched my interests.

If I had to sum up the essence of this book in just a few words, I would say it like this: Find out what people have on their minds and connect with them there.

You can always break their preoccupation with a shocking statement or action (or gift), but you can befriend them quicker if you merge with their dominate thoughts and concerns. From there, they will follow your lead. But rapport has to come first. As I've said many times, people buy only from people they know, they like, and they respect.

Think about the two gifts I received and my responses to them. That, in essence, is the secret of the Buying Trance.

BONUS SPECIAL REPORT

I asked Blair Warren, a television producer and reclusive persuasion expert, if he would give me permission to include this remarkable special report. I believe that his "one sentence" for persuasion can help you understand how to create a Buying Trance in your prospects. The idea is to use one or more of the elements in his 27-word sentence to get people's attention and get your message through. Blair gave his permission and here's his report. Enjoy.

The One-Sentence Persuasion Course: 27 Words to Make the World Do Your Bidding
Blair Warren

ONE-SENTENCE PERSUASION?

Is it possible to capture and communicate anything of value about persuasion in a single sentence? It is and I'm about to prove it. But first, let me tell you why I've gone to this extreme.

Studying persuasion and influence is one of my deepest passions and has consumed an embarrassingly large amount of my time and energy for over a decade. I have family and friends who say my pursuit borders on obsession. They are wrong. It crossed the line long ago.

I know of no subject more fascinating, more empowering, more profitable, and, unfortunately, more confusing. This confusion is more than unfortunate; it is also largely unnecessary. Given the pace of today's world, it has never been easier to be powerfully persuasive. Never. It doesn't require good looks, a silver tongue, or infallible logic. It doesn't require confidence, charisma, or a magnetic personality. It is a simple matter when one cuts through all the smoke. Cutting through the smoke is the hard part. In fact, if you have yet to develop your persuasive powers to the level you want, it likely has nothing to do with you. Given the shell game of strategies and misinformation available, it is a wonder we're still able to understand each other, much less persuade each other.

If this barrage of techno-jargon has left you more confused than empowered, take a deep breath and relax. We're about to take aim at this confusion, blow away the smoke, and make things as simple as possible. In fact, we'll nail it down to a single sentence: just 27 words. And with these words we can work miracles.

But first, we must clear away some smoke.

THE SETUP

Before we venture into our material on persuasion, let's take a quick peek at the field of magic, for the two share a common core.

Try this sometime:

Visit a magic shop in your city and spend a half hour or so watching the owner demonstrate some tricks. Pick the one that baffles you the most and buy it. Then go out to your car, open up the instructions (if you're like me, you won't be able to wait till you get home), and discover how the trick works. If you will do this, I can predict with 99.9 percent accuracy what will happen.

You will be disappointed.

The secrets behind many magic tricks, even some of those that seem like miracles, are often so mundane that one cannot help but feel disappointed upon their discovery. Now for another prediction: Your next thought will be,

"This is ridiculous. This wouldn't fool anyone."

At this point, if you're like most people, you'll put the trick away and consider your $20 investment a bust. But if you're honest with yourself (and few people are), you will have another thought that can transform the way you look at life. No joke. That thought goes something like this:

"Wait a minute. It must not be *that* ridiculous if it fooled *me*."

And with this one thought you will have risen to a level of intellectual honesty and understanding that few people ever experience; you will have discovered that the most magical things in life—*on and off the stage*—are often the result of the correct application of the most basic principles imaginable.

This is perhaps nowhere more true than in the field of persuasion. I realize this is heresy for me to say, as persuasion is clearly a complicated field. And judging from the amount of new material coming out every day, it's only going to get more so. Without a doubt it has never been easier for us to get lost down the rabbit hole, only to be spit back out more confused and broke than when we started.

As someone who has studied these materials for many years I'll be the first to tell you there is a lot of great stuff out there. Many subtleties and distinctions are available that can have a powerful impact on our ability to persuade others. Unfortunately, for every one of these, there are a dozen nuances that only serve to complicate and confuse.

The good news is one does not have to spend years studying this type of material to become an almost frighteningly powerful persuader. If you find this hard to believe, consider that charismatic leaders and hypnotic seducers have been around as long as there have been people to lead and to seduce. If *they* didn't need today's cutting-edge techniques, why do you?

Yes, these ideas *can* help, and if you are hell-bent on maximizing your skills, you should become familiar with them all. But don't let anyone tell you they are necessary in order to have a powerful impact on others.

What *is* necessary is a fundamental understanding of human nature, for persuasion—even the most extreme examples of persuasion such as suicide cults and mass movements—are often based on the most basic of human desires. Just as magicians can perform miracles using mundane principles, powerful persuaders shape the world in much the same way.

So we are left with basics. The question now becomes, *which* basics? I am sure if you asked this question of 100 different persuasion experts, you'd get 100 different answers.

But I'm also certain there would be much common ground. I am certain of this because I have seen it *hiding* behind the varied terminologies and philosophies in their materials. When one strips away the jargon and intricacies of the material available, one is left with some very basic, very powerful understandings. And while each of us might represent these in different ways, the important thing is to get a handle on them so that they are available at a moment's notice.

THE SENTENCE

I have found the best way to do this is to encapsulate these understandings in a single sentence. Not a sentence that one *delivers*, but a sentence that one *remembers*. A sentence that can help guide your efforts from beginning to end in virtually every situation imaginable. This sentence could easily be condensed or expanded, and after reading this report I encourage you to try to do this for yourself. In fact, the best way to make these ideas your own is to modify them to suit your own understanding and experiences. But we're getting ahead of ourselves here. Let's look at this sentence—this "one-sentence persuasion course"—and see what makes it tick. Here it is:

People will do anything for those who encourage their dreams, justify their failures, allay their fears, confirm their suspicions, and help them throw rocks at their enemies.

Read that again:

People will do anything for those who encourage their dreams, justify their failures, allay their fears, confirm their suspicions, and help them throw rocks at their enemies.

That, in a single sentence, contains five of the most important insights I have learned in all my years of studying and applying the principles of persuasion:

1. Encourage their dreams.
2. Justify their failures.
3. Allay their fears.
4. Confirm their suspicions.
5. Help them throw rocks at their enemies.

Now, these insights are not the most important because they are comprehensive—they aren't. They're not the most important because they've been scientifically proven—they haven't. And they're not the most important because they're based on the latest "persuasion technology"—they're not. They are the most important because they are simple, they are immediately useful, and they can be almost frighteningly powerful.

Adolph Hitler used them and nearly took over the world. Cult leaders Jim Jones, David Koresh, and Marshall Applewhite used them and commanded such loyalty that many of their followers willingly—*even eagerly*—died for them.

And yet, these five insights are tools not only for madmen, but for marketers, salesmen, seducers, evangelists, entertainers, and others. In short, they are the tools for anyone who must connect with others and, more importantly, make these connections pay off.

THE EXPLANATION

If you don't believe me, try to find a truly successful ad campaign that does not use one or more of these five insights. Really, try to find one. Then, when you give up on that, try finding a deep, satisfying relationship that isn't built upon one or more of them. Just try to find people who have a remarkable chemistry yet fail to encourage each other's dreams. Or who demand that the other is to blame. Or who fail to address each other's concerns. Or who treat each other as paranoid. Or who leave each other to fight their own battles. While I'm sure you could find an example if you searched hard enough, I am also certain that for every one you find, I can find a hundred to counter it. The bottom line is, whenever and wherever people form powerful bonds, these insights are more often than not lurking in the shadows.

Now there is nothing particularly difficult to understand about these strategies. They are self-explanatory. Some may even say obvious. But to dismiss them on these grounds is an enormous mistake. In fact, dismissing them is one reason they are even more powerful for those who do not dismiss them.

Think back to our trip to the magic shop and how quick we

were to dismiss the secret behind our little trick. And yet, magicians aren't so quick to dismiss. Instead, they take these simple secrets that "wouldn't fool anybody" and build upon them to create illusions that baffle the most brilliant among us. It is much the same with powerful persuasion. Its effects can be so sudden, so dramatic, so life-altering that we remain convinced there has to be something deeper, something more complex, going on. More often than not, there isn't. There is simply the correct application of very basic principles by people who appreciate their power. And since the rest of us dismiss these principles as being too basic and too obvious to work, we flounder in complexity and minutiae that sound great on paper but fall flat in practice.

But by overlooking the power of these basic principles, we do more than guarantee ourselves failure and frustration: We leave those with whom we wish to connect vulnerable to others who may fill these needs we so casually dismiss.

Consider the following.

On encouraging their dreams . . .
Parents often discourage their children's dreams "for their own good" and attempt to steer them toward more "reasonable" goals. And children often accept this as normal until others come along who believe in them and encourage their dreams. When this happens, who do you think has more power? Parents or strangers?

On justifying their failures . . .
While millions cheer Dr. Phil as he tells people to accept responsibility for their mistakes, millions more are looking for someone to take the responsibility *off* their shoulders—to tell them that they are not responsible for their lot in life. And while accepting responsibility is essential for gaining control of one's own life, assuring others *they are not responsible* is essential for gaining influence over theirs. One need look no

further than politics to see this powerful game played at its best.

On allaying their fears . . .
When we are afraid, it is almost impossible to concentrate on anything else. And while everyone knows this, what do we do when someone else is afraid and we need to get their attention? That's right. We tell them not to be afraid and expect that to do the trick. Does it work? Hardly. And yet we don't seem to notice. We go on as if we'd solved the problem and the person before us fades further away.

But there are those who *do* realize this and pay special attention to our fears. They do not tell us not to be afraid. They work with us until our fear subsides. They present evidence. They offer support. They tell us stories. But they do not tell us how to feel and expect us to feel that way. When you are afraid, which type of person do you prefer to be with?

On confirming their suspicions . . .
One of our favorite things to say is "I knew it." There is just nothing quite like having our suspicions confirmed. When another person confirms something that we suspect, we not only feel a surge of superiority, we feel attracted to the one who helped make that surge come about. Hitler "confirmed" the suspicions of many Germans about the cause of their troubles and drew them further into his power by doing so. Cults often confirm the suspicions of prospective members by telling them that their families are out to sabotage them. It is a simple thing to confirm the suspicions of those who are desperate to believe them.

And finally, on helping them throw rocks at their enemies . . .
Nothing bonds like having a common enemy. I realize how ugly this sounds, yet it is true just the same. Those who understand this can utilize this. Those who don't under-

stand it or, even worse, understand but refuse to address it are throwing away one of the most effective ways of connecting with others. No matter what you may think of this, rest assured that people have enemies. All people. It has been said that everyone you meet is engaged in a great struggle. The thing they are struggling with is their enemy. Whether it is another individual, a group, an illness, a setback, a rival philosophy or religion, or what have you, when you are engaged in a struggle, you are looking for others to join your side. Those who do become more than friends. They become partners.

While these insights seem like common sense, they are anything but common practice—except among master persuaders.

WHAT'S MISSING?

There is something else worth noting about this sentence. It is missing something most people think is very important in the persuasion process. Read the sentence again and see if you can tell what it is:

> **People will do anything for those who encourage their dreams, justify their failures, allay their fears, confirm their suspicions, and help them throw rocks at their enemies.**

Any ideas? If so, you're one step ahead of the game. Here's what's missing: *you*. There isn't a word about *your* wants, *your* needs, *your* hopes, or *your* concerns. There isn't a word about *your* offer or proposal. There isn't a word about what *you* think. It is all about what the other person does.

Again, this is heresy. People write books about how to frame *your* ideas, how to present *your*self, how to put *your* best foot forward. And yet, all that people really care about is themselves. Can you imagine how much energy you will free up if you stop focusing on yourself and put your attention on other people? Can you even imagine how much more charismatic you will become when you come to be seen as the one who can fulfill some of their most basic emotional needs?

Think of it like this:

Imagine you are sitting down with someone you hope to influence. Your proposal makes sense. Your arguments are solid. The conversation is even pleasant. But the entire time *you are looking off to the side, not at the person*. Now, how much of a connection do you think you are going to make with that person? Remember, everything is perfect with the exception of your focus. Your message shines. Your confidence is solid. Your proposal is a no-brainer. And yet, none of this makes the slightest bit of difference when you are looking *past* the other person. This is exactly what happens in a conversation when your focus is on your own goals.

You are looking *past* the person and everything that is most important to them, and you have little hope of ever being able to establish a deep connection. Still not convinced? Then notice what else our sentence doesn't say. It does not say people will do anything for those who educate them, do what's best for them, or even treat them fairly. It does not say people will do anything for those who are eloquent, well-dressed, and pleasant, nor those who make the best case for their proposals, who are reasonable, and come across as intelligent.

When we focus on the basic principles of human nature *these things become negligible*. When we focus on the basic principles of human nature, we create relationships in which people *naturally* want to do things for us. *This* is the real secret to getting what we want. Really. It is that simple. Or, I should say, it *can* be that simple.

Have you ever noticed that the harder you push, the more resistance you get? When you focus on what you want, people will resist. That's what people do. Politicians lie, the sun rises in the east, and people resist pressure. But one thing people rarely resist is someone trying to meet their needs. And when one's needs have been met a bond is often forged and a natural desire to reciprocate has been created. And just how powerful is this desire? To what extremes will people go to repay the favor? This is the frightening part. But don't take my word for it. Look around and see for yourself.

People willingly leave their families for cults that fulfill these needs for them. People pick up arms and kill others for those who meet their deepest needs. People leave long-term marriages and relationships for people they just met and their spouses are often left stunned. They wouldn't be if they understood the power of these needs. Like it or not, the duration of our relationships is nothing compared to the *depth* of our relationships. And depth is based on the fulfillment of our deepest needs, not on the duration of dialogue. Notice I have never said you should *ignore* your wants. I simply said you should focus on the other person, not forget yourself. Or to be more specific, when you are with a person you want to influence, your primary focus should be on that person. Do not look past him or her by focusing on your intentions.

The time to focus on your own hopes, dreams, and desires is when you're alone. This is when you should get clear on what you hope to accomplish, on what you would like to occur, in any given encounter. But once you get this state of clarity and find yourself face-to-face with another, place your attention where it can have the greatest impact. Place it on the other person. Don't be afraid that your wishes will go unnoticed. On the contrary, they will find a way to express themselves in your encounters. Whether they arise spontaneously or the other solicits them, they will arise naturally. And when they arise naturally, they are often fulfilled effortlessly.

EXAMPLES

As I said earlier, there is nothing particularly difficult to understand about these strategies, especially when it comes to one-on-one encounters. But how might they be used in other contexts, such as web sites and advertising? And can they have the same impact they would in an interpersonal encounter?

The answer to the first question is, easily. The answer to the second is, absolutely. For example:

Example 1: Pelmanism

Recently my friends Joe Vitale and Pat O'Bryan launched a web site that unexpectedly shattered sales records. The success of the site surprised everyone involved and there was much discussion as to why it was so effective.

Was it the product? Was it the price? Was it just the right offer at the right time? I'm sure each of these things played a role, but I know something else that played a role as well: The copy spoke to some very basic human needs—needs that we have been discussing in this special report. For example, the headline reads:

> "If You're the Kind Of Person Who Wants to Break Free from Limited Thinking and Finally Get Whatever You Want in Life . . . These 12 Long-Lost Astonishing Books Written in the 1920s Will Set You Free!"

This clearly encourages our dreams of freedom, of getting what we want. This is literally the first line of their letter and they've already struck a powerful vein of influence. Let's look at the next paragraph. It reads:

> We feel your pain. You've read *Think and Grow Rich*. You've scoured the shelves in bookstores for hours trying to find something that will answer the one question that has haunted you for years: "Why am I not where I want to be financially, mentally, or spiritually?" You've done everything that you can . . . but there's still something holding you back.

This paragraph not only lets us know they recognize our frustration (i.e., "We feel your pain"), but it suggests that *it isn't our fault*. While we've done "everything" that we can, there is still "something" holding us back. So the answer lies with this mysterious "something" and not with us. Not only are they letting us off the hook, but they're about to confirm our suspicion that there is an answer to our dilemma. And in the next section, they introduce us to it:

What is it?

> For years, people just like you have asked this same question. Fortunately for some, they were able to get the answer to this, and many other questions, by purchasing a course back in the 1920s. If you were to flip through some of the magazines and newspapers back then, you would have seen some of the world's first direct response ads. What were the ads for?
>
> Pelmanism.

And there it is: confirmation that an answer to our problems exists. It's called Pelmanism. In just a few short paragraphs they have managed to address three of the five insights we've been discussing. And from this point on, their readers are hooked. To see for yourself, read the full letter at www.pelmanismonline.com. It is well worth studying.

Just how successful has this site been? In Joe's own words, they "sold hundreds of copies . . . and saw about $9,000 appear almost instantly." Not bad for a site they spent little time creating. Again, when our needs are being addressed, we don't care if the copy is slick, if the graphics look great, or even if the site is easy to navigate. We look past the superficial and listen deeply to those who speak to us.

Example 2: Depression, Weight Loss, and Landscaping

One of the most common of our five insights is justifying the failure of others. In my *Forbidden Keys to Persuasion* material I refer to this as "scapegoating." While the terminology is different, the underlying principle is the same. Here is an excerpt from my *Forbidden Keys* material that illustrates the power of this insight:

> A couple of television commercials that are currently airing in the United States . . . brilliantly and ethically employ the concept of scapegoating and they do so at the very beginning of their scripts.
>
> The first commercial, for an antidepressant medication, starts out with something like, "Feeling depressed lately? It may be the result of a chemical imbalance in your brain." The second commercial, one for a weight loss product, starts out like this: "If you've tried to lose that extra weight and have failed, it may not be your fault. It may be your metabolism."
>
> Can you see their use of the scapegoat principle? If you're depressed, *it may not be your fault*. It might simply be a biological factor beyond your control. And if you're overweight and have failed to slim down, *it might not be your fault*, but simply a problem with your metabolism! What makes the use of scapegoating in these situations ethical is that they are absolutely true statements. Depression *can* be caused by a chemical imbalance in the brain. And obesity *can* be caused by metabolism. What makes the use of scapegoating brilliant in these cases is that it is used immediately in the pitches and instantly offers the viewer something of value—a scapegoat for their problems. From here, the viewer is much more open to the rest of the message.

A friend of mine who is a landscaper once told me that when he first meets potential clients they are often embarrassed by the condition of their property. When he senses this, he immediately points out how many of the problems with their property are due to such things as drought conditions, bad soil conditions, and the like. In other words, the condition of their property doesn't say anything negative about the potential client.

It isn't their fault! How important is this subtle change in strategy? He told me that the number of people he secured as clients increased significantly once he realized that people want their property to look nicer, but often don't want to accept responsibility for it looking poor in the first place.

Example 3: This Special Report

If I've held your attention thus far, there's a good reason for it: I have used the one-sentence strategy in writing this very report. If you'll go back and reread it, you will find places I've used our five insights sprinkled throughout. However, the best example is the second half of the opening section itself, "One-Sentence Persuasion?" I closed that section using each of our five insights to not only demonstrate the effectiveness of these ideas, but also to give you a sense of how powerful and *transparent* they can be.

Let's look at some of that section and see how I worked each of these insights into it without raising an eyebrow.

The first paragraph reads:

> Given the pace of today's world, it has never been easier to be powerfully persuasive. Never. It doesn't require good looks, a silver tongue, or infallible logic. It doesn't require confidence, charisma, or a magnetic personality. It is a simple matter when one cuts through all the smoke. Cutting through the smoke is the hard part.

Here, I am encouraging the reader's dreams of becoming more persuasive. And for those who have doubts about their potential (e.g., not enough confidence, charisma, etc.), I take extra steps to assure them they can do it as well.

The next paragraph reads:

> In fact, if you have yet to develop your persuasive powers to the level you want, it likely has nothing to do with you. Given the shell game of strategies and misinformation available, it is a wonder we're still able to understand each other, much less persuade each other.

In this paragraph I address two of our insights. First, I justify the failure of readers for not already being persuasive enough. Second, I confirm their suspicions that much of the available material is too complex and confusing for anyone to understand.

And the final paragraph reads:

> If this barrage of techno-jargon has left you more confused than empowered, take a deep breath and relax. We're about to take aim at this confusion, blow away the smoke, and make things as simple as possible. In fact, we'll nail it down to a single sentence: just 27 words. And with these words we can work miracles. But first, we must clear away some smoke.

Here, I complete the task by allaying their fears (i.e., "take a deep breath and relax") and helping them throw rocks at their enemies (i.e., "We're about to take aim"). And notice my use of the term *we*. I said, *"We're* about to take aim," not *"I'm* about to take aim." I then said that *"we* must clear away some smoke," not *"I* must clear away some smoke." This helps assure readers that I'm on *their* side.

There are two important lessons to take away from this example. First, as I said before, these insights were *seamlessly* integrated into this report. They do not stand out as being too obvious or simple because they aren't. In fact, since they do not stand out they are all the more powerful. And second, my use of these insights is *authentic*. I didn't have to fabricate these statements to make them fit this strategy. Yes, I phrased them as I did with our insights in mind. But they remain grounded in truth—an essential factor if we are to avoid getting our way but hating ourselves in the morning.

These three examples illustrate how widespread and applicable these insights really are. While most people like to think they are too wise to fall for such tactics, this very thinking makes them just that much more susceptible. One need only consider how successful these types of approaches are to confirm this.

NOW WHAT?

Friedrich Nietzsche reportedly said that the message of most books could be reduced to a single paragraph without losing anything of value. In this report I have attempted to go one better: I have tried to create an entire "persuasion course" in a single sentence.

I will be the first to admit that by doing this I have, in fact, left out many things that could be of value to the would-be persuader. But as I said at the outset, if there is one thing I know to be true, it is that the most magical things in life—*on and off the stage*—are often the result of the correct application of the most basic principles imaginable. And I have found few principles that are more basic and more powerful than those offered in this one sentence:

> People will do anything for those who encourage their dreams, justify their failures, allay their fears, confirm their suspicions, and help them throw rocks at their enemies.

So my goal in this report wasn't to give you a comprehensive plan to follow. It was to simplify a process that is often needlessly complex. It was to clear away cumbersome techniques and strategies that often serve to separate more than persuade. And ultimately, it was to provide a core concept you can use to build relationships that are not only powerful, but profitable.

Whether you find this notion distasteful or not, there is one thing you can count on: Your family, friends, customers, clients, and even everyone you have yet to meet will have these needs met by someone. The only question is, will it be by you?

Blair Warren is a television producer, writer, marketing consultant, and voracious student of human nature. He is the creator of *The Forbidden Keys to Persuasion E-Class* and the author of *The No-Nonsense Guide to Enlightenment* and is currently working on his next book, *Spontaneous Persuasion: Getting What You Want by Simply Being Who You Are*. To read more of Blair's material and get more information on his work, visit his web site at www.blairwarren.com.

Bibliography

Ackoff, Russell L., Jason Magidson, and Herbert Addison. *Idealized Design: How to Dissolve Tomorrow's Crisis . . . Today.* Upper Saddle River, NJ: Wharton School Publishing, 2006.

Adams, Mike. *Spam Filters for Your Brain: How to Navigate through the Lies, Hype and Mind Games of the Food, Drug and Cosmetic Industries.* Tucson, AZ: Truth Publishing, 2006.

Adams, Mike, and Alexis Black. *The Real Safety Guide to Protecting against Advertisers, Marketers and Big Business Propaganda.* Tucson, AZ: Truth Publishing, 2006.

Anderson, Chris. *The Long Tail: Why the Future of Business Is Selling Less of More.* New York: Hyperion, 2006.

Andreas, Steve. *Six Blind Elephants: Understanding Ourselves and Each Other.* 2 vols. Vol. 1, *Fundamental Principles of Scope and Category.* Vol. 2, *Applications and Explorations of Scope and Category.* Moab, UT: Real People Press, 2006.

Anonymous. *Dynamic Speed Hypnosis.* Escondido, CA: The Master Hypnotist, 1956.

Alsop, Ronald. *The* Wall Street Journal *on Marketing.* New York: New American Library, 1986.

Bacon, Mark. *Write Like the Pros: Using the Secrets of Ad Writers and Journalists in Business.* New York: John Wiley & Sons, 1988.

Baker, Nan, Cathy Greenberg, and Collins Hemingway. *What Happy Companies Know: How the New Science of Happiness Can Change Your Company for the Better.* Upper Saddle River, NJ: Pearson Education, 2006.

Bandler, Richard, and John Grinder. *Frogs into Princes: Neuro-Linguistic Programming*. Moab, UT: Real People Press, 1979.

———. *The Structure of Magic: A Book about Language and Therapy*. Palo Alto, CA: Science & Behavior Books, 1975.

———. *Trance-Formations: Neuro-Linguistic Programming and the Structure of Hypnosis*. Moab, UT: Real People Press, 1981.

Bauer, Joel, and Mark Levy. *How to Persuade People Who Don't Want to Be Persuaded: Get What You Want Every Time*. Hoboken, NJ: John Wiley & Sons, 2004.

Beck, Don Edward, and Christopher Cowan. *Spiral Dynamics: Mastering Values, Leadership, and Change*. Malden, MA: Blackwell, 2006.

Blakeslee, Thomas. *Beyond the Conscious Mind: Unlocking the Secrets of the Self*. Lincoln, NE: iUniverse, 1996.

Block, Lawrence. *Write for Your Life: The Book about the Seminar*. Ft. Myers Beach, FL: Write for Your Life, 1986.

Boyce, Oren Douglas. *The Power of Indirect Hypnosis: Hypnosis, Genetics, and Depression*. New York: Vantage Press, 1999.

Brown, Peter. *The Hypnotic Brain: Hypnotherapy and Social Communication*. New Haven, CT: Yale University Press, 1991.

Burton, John. *Hypnotic Language: Its Structure and Use*. Carmarthen, UK: Crown House, 2000.

———. *States of Equilibrium*. Carmarthen, UK: Crown House, 2003.

Caples, John. *How to Make Your Advertising Make Money*. Englewood Cliffs, NJ: Prentice-Hall, 1983.

———. *Tested Advertising Methods*. Englewood Cliffs, NJ: Prentice-Hall, 1974.

Carpenter, Harry. *The Genie Within: Your Subconscious Mind*. San Diego, CA: Anaphase II Publishing, 2004.

Carr, Allen. *The Easy Way to Stop Smoking*. New York: Sterling, 2004.

Chafetz, Morris. *Big Fat Liars: How Politicians, Corporations, and the Media Use Science and Statistics to Manipulate the Public*. New York: Nelson Current, 2005.

Charvet, Shelle Rose. *Words That Change Minds: Mastering the Language of Influence*. Dubuque, IA: Kendall/Hunt, 1995.

Chisnall, Peter. *Consumer Behaviour*. London: McGraw-Hill, 1975.

Cloud, Michael. *Secrets of Libertarian Persuasion: Discover the Keys to Opening People's Hearts and Minds to Liberty*. Cartersville, GA: Advocates for Self-Government, 2004.

Cohen, Marshal. *Why Customers Do What They Do*. New York: McGraw-Hill, 2006.

Cohen, Steve. *Win the Crowd: Unlock the Secrets of Influence, Charisma, and Showmanship*. New York: Collins, 2005.

Collier, Robert. *The Robert Collier Letter Book*. Oak Harbor, WA: Robert Collier Publications, 1937.

———. *The Secret of the Ages*. Oak Harbor, WA: Robert Collier Publications, 1960.

Conklin, Robert. *How to Get People to Do Things*. Chicago: Contemporary Books, 1979.

———. *The Power of a Magnetic Personality*. New York: Parker, 1965.

Considine, Ray, and Murray Raphel. *The Great Brain Robbery: A Collection of Proven Ideas to Make Money and Change Your Life*. Altadena, CA: Great Brain Robbery, 1980.

Dillard, James Price, and Michael Pfau. *The Persuasion Handbook: Developments in Theory and Practice*. London: Sage Publications, 2002.

Dolan, Yvonne. *A Path with a Heart: Ericksonian Utilization with Resistant and Chronic Clients*. New York: Brunner/Mazel, 1985.

Du Plessis, Erik. *The Advertised Mind: Ground-Breaking Insights into How Our Brains Respond to Advertising*. London: Kogan Page, 2005.

Dweck, Carol. *Mindset: The New Psychology of Success*. New York: Random House, 2006.

Edmonston, William, Jr. *The Induction of Hypnosis*. New York: John Wiley & Sons, 1986.

Eisenberg, Bryan, and Jeffrey Eisenberg. *Waiting for Your Cat to Bark? Persuading Customers When They Ignore Marketing*. New York: Nelson Business, 2006.

Elman, Dave. *Hypnotherapy*. Glendale, CA: Westwood Publishing, 1964.

Erickson, Betty Alice. *Milton H. Erickson, M.D.: An American Healer*. Sedona, AZ: Ringling Rocks Press, 2006.

Erickson, Milton H. *The Nature of Hypnosis and Suggestion: The Collected Papers of Milton H. Erickson on Hypnosis*, Vol. 1. New York: Irvington, 1980.

Estabrooks, George. *Hypnotism*. New York: Dutton, 1943.

Faludi, Susan. *Backlash: The Undeclared War against American Women*. New York: Anchor, 1992.

Fisk, Peter. *Marketing Genius*. West Sussex, England: Capstone, 2006.

Flesch, Rudolf. *The Art of Readable Writing*. New York: Harper & Row, 1959.

Foxall, Gordon. *Marketing Psychology: The Paradigm in the Wings*. New York: Palgrave, 1997.

Frankel, Fred. *Hypnosis: Trance as a Coping Mechanism*. New York: Plenum, 1976.

Fritz, Robert. *Creating*. New York: Ballantine, 1993.

———. *The Path of Least Resistance*. New York: Ballantine, 1989.

Fromm, Erika. *Contemporary Hypnosis Research*. New York: Guilford Press, 1992.

Gafner, George. *Hypnotic Techniques for Standard Psychotherapy and Formal Hypnosis*. New York: Norton, 2003.

Gallwey, Timothy. *The Inner Game of Tennis*. New York: Random House, 1997.

Garfinkel, David. *Advertising Headlines that Make You Rich.* Garden City, NY: Morgan James, 2006.

Garn, Roy. *The Magic Power of Emotional Appeal.* Englewood Cliffs, NJ: Prentice-Hall, 1960.

Gauld, Alan. *A History of Hypnotism.* New York: Cambridge University Press, 1992.

Gilligan, Stephen. *Therapeutic Trances: The Cooperation Principle in Ericksonian Hypnotherapy.* Levittown, PA: Brunner/ Mazel, 1987.

Glassner, Selma. *The Analogy Book of Related Words: Your Secret Shortcut to Power Writing.* Buena Vista, CO: Communication Creativity, 1990.

Godefroy, Christian. *How to Write Letters That Sell: Winning Techniques for Achieving Sales through Direct Mail.* London: Piatkus, 1994.

Godin, Seth. *All Marketers Are Liars: The Power of Telling Authentic Stories in a Low-Trust World.* New York: Portfolio/ Penguin, 2005.

Goode, Kenneth. *Advertising.* New York: Greenberg, 1932.

Goodwin, James. *A History of Modern Psychology.* Hoboken, NJ: John Wiley & Sons, 2005.

Gordon, David. *Phoenix: Therapeutic Metaphors.* Cupertino, CA: Meta, 1978.

———. *Therapeutic Patterns of Milton H. Erickson.* Cupertino, CA: Meta Publications, 1981.

Grambs, David. *The Describer's Dictionary.* New York: Norton, 1993.

Green, Barry, and Timothy Gallwey. *The Inner Game of Music.* New York: Doubleday, 1986.

Gross, John. *The Oxford Book of Aphorisms.* New York: Oxford University Press, 1987.

Grothe, Mardy. *Never Let a Fool Kiss You or a Kiss Fool You: Word Play for Word Lovers.* New York: Penguin, 1999.

Haddock, Frank Channing. *Power of Will.* Robert Collier Publishing, 1979.

Haley, Jay. *Jay Haley on Milton H. Erickson*. Bristol, PA: Brunner/ Mazel, 1993.

Hammond, Corydon. *Handbook of Hypnotic Suggestions and Metaphors*. New York: Norton, 1990.

Hatch, Denison. *Million Dollar Mailings*. Washington, DC: Libey Publishing, 1992.

Hattwick, Mel. *The New Psychology of Selling*. New York: McGraw-Hill, 1960.

Havens, Ronald. *The Wisdom of Milton H. Erickson: The Complete Volume*. Carmarthen, UK: Crown House, 2003.

Heller, Steven. *Monsters and Magical Sticks: There's No Such Thing as Hypnosis?* Tempe, AZ: New Falcon, 1987.

Hilgard, Ernest. *Hypnotic Susceptibility*. New York: Harcourt, Brace & World, 1965.

Hill, Dan. *Body of Truth: Leveraging What Consumers Can't or Won't Say*. Hoboken, NJ: John Wiley & Sons, 2003.

Hodge, Richard. *The Mind of the Customer*. New York: McGraw-Hill, 2006.

Hogan, Kevin. *Covert Hypnosis*. Eagan, MN: Network 3000, 2001.

———. *The Psychology of Persuasion: How to Persuade Others to Your Way of Thinking*. Gretna, LA: Pelican, 1996.

———. *The Science of Influence: How to Get Anyone to Say Yes in 8 Minutes or Less*. Hoboken, NJ: John Wiley & Sons, 2005.

———. *Through the Open Door: Secrets of Self-Hypnosis*. Gretna LA: Pelican, 2000.

Honek, Water. *My Amazing Discovery*. Austin, TX: Beta Books, 1993.

Howard, John. *The Theory of Buyer Behavior*. New York: John Wiley & Sons, 1969.

Howard, Pierce. *The Owner's Manual for the Brain: Everyday Applications from Mind-Brain Research*. Austin, TX: Bard Press, 2000.

Izard, Carroll. *The Psychology of Emotions*. New York: Plenum, 1991.

Jacobson, J. Z. *Scott of Northwestern: The Life Story of a Pioneer in Psychology and Education*. Chicago: Mariano, 1951.

James, William. *The Principles of Psychology*. New York: Dover, 1950.

Joyner, Mark. *The Great Formula: For Creating Maximum Profit with Minimal Effort*. Hoboken, NJ: John Wiley & Sons, 2006.

————. *The Irresistible Offer: How to Sell Your Product or Service in 3 Seconds or Less*. Hoboken, NJ: John Wiley & Sons, 2005.

Keeney, Bradford. *Aesthetics of Change*. New York: Guilford Press, 1983.

————. *Improvisational Therapy: A Practical Guide for Creative Clinical Strategies*. New York: Guilford Press, 1990.

Kennedy, Dan. *The Ultimate Sales Letter*. Holbrook, MA: Adams Media, 1990.

Kilstein, Harlan. *Steal This Book! Million Dollar Sales Letters You Can Legally Steal to Suck in Cash like a Vacuum on Steroids*. Garden City, NY: Morgan James, 2006.

Kocina, Lonny. *Media Hypnosis: Unleashing the Most Powerful Sales Tool on Earth*. Minneapolis, MN: Mid-America Entertainment, 2002.

Lakhani, Dave. *Persuasion: The Art of Getting What You Want*. Hoboken, NJ: John Wiley & Sons, 2005.

————. *Power of an Hour*. Hoboken, NJ: John Wiley & Sons, 2006.

Ledochowski, Igor. *The Deep Trance Training Manual*, Vol. 1. Carmarthen, UK: Crown House, 2003.

Lempert, Phil. *Being the Shopper: Understanding the Buyer's Choice*. Hoboken, NJ: John Wiley & Sons, 2002.

Lentz, John. *How the Word Heals: Hypnosis in Scriptures*. Lincoln, NE: iUniverse, 2002.

Levy, Mark. *The Accidental Genius: Revolutionize Your Thinking through Private Writing*. San Francisco: Berrett-Koehler, 2000.

Martineau, Pierre. *Motivation in Advertising: Motives That Make People Buy*. New York: McGraw-Hill, 1957.

McGill, Ormond. *The New Encyclopedia of Stage Hypnotism.* Carmarthen, UK: Crown House, 1996.

McKee, Robert. *Story: Substance, Structure, Style, and the Principles of Screenwriting.* New York: ReganBooks/HarperCollins, 1997.

McLauchlin, Larry. *Advanced Language Patterns Mastery.* Calgary, Canada: Leading Edge Communications, 1992.

McMillan, John. *Reinventing the Bazaar: A Natural History of Markets.* New York: Norton, 2002.

McNeilly, Robert, and Jenny Brown. *Healing with Words.* Australia: Hill of Content, 1994.

Miller, Anne. *Metaphorically Selling: How to Use the Magic of Metaphors to Sell, Persuade and Explain Anything to Anyone.* New York: Chiron Associates, 2004.

Moine, Donald. *Unlimited Selling Power: How to Master Hypnotic Selling Skills.* Upper Saddle River, NJ: Prentice-Hall, 1990.

Monk, Gerald. *Narrative Therapy in Practice: The Archaeology of Hope.* San Francisco: Jossey-Bass, 1997.

Mullen, Brian. *The Psychology of Human Behavior.* Mahwah, NJ: Lawrence Erlbaum, 1990.

Murphy, Gardner. *An Outline of Abnormal Psychology.* New York: Modern Library, 1929.

Nicholas, Ted. *How to Turn Words into Money.* Indian Rocks Beach, FL, 2004.

O'Hanlon, William Hudson. *Solution-Oriented Hypnosis: An Ericksonian Approach.* New York: Norton, 1992.

O'Shaughnessy, John. *Why People Buy.* New York: Oxford University Press, 1987.

Overdurf, John. *Training Trances: Multi-Level Communication in Therapy and Training.* Portland, OR: Metamorphous Press, 1994.

Petrie, Sidney, and Robert Stone. *How to Strengthen Your Life with Mental Isometrics.* New York: Parker, 1967.

Plous, Scott. *The Psychology of Judgment and Decision Making.* New York: McGraw-Hill, 1993.

Price, Jonathan, and Lisa Price. *Hot Text: Web Writing That Works.* Indianapolis, IN: NewRiders, 2002.

Rapaille, Clotaire. *The Culture Code: An Ingenious Way to Understand Why People Around the World Live and Buy as They Do.* New York: Broadway Books, 2006.

Reiss, Steven. *Who Am I? The 16 Basic Desires That Motivate Our Actions and Define Our Personalities.* New York: Berkley, 2000.

Restak, Richard M. *The New Brain: How the Modern Age Is Rewiring Your Mind.* Emmaus, PA: Rodale, 2003.

Rosen, Sidney. *My Voice Will Go with You: The Teaching Tales of Milton H. Erickson.* New York: Norton, 1982.

Rubleski, Tony. *Mind Capture: How to Stand Out in the Age of Advertising Overload.* Hampton Roads, VA: Morgan James, 2006.

Sant, Tom. *The Giants of Sales: What Dale Carnegie, John Patterson, Elmer Wheeler, and Joe Girard Can Teach You about Real Sales Success.* New York: Amacom, 2006.

Sarno, John. *The Divided Mind: The Epidemic of Mindbody Disorders.* New York: ReganBooks/HarperCollins, 2006.

Schank, Roger. *Tell Me a Story: Narrative and Intelligence.* Evanston, IL: Northwestern University Press, 1995.

Schwab, Victor. *How to Write a Good Advertisement: A Short Course in Copywriting.* Hollywood, CA: Wilshire Books, 1962.

Schwartz, Eugene. *Breakthrough Advertising.* Stamford, CT: Bottom Line Books, 2004.

Scott, Walter Dill. *Influencing Men in Business.* New York: Ronald Press, 1911.

———. *The Psychology of Advertising.* Boston: Small, Maynard, 1913.

————. *The Theory of Advertising*. Boston: Small, Maynard, 1903.

Shazer, Steve de. *Words Were Originally Magic*. New York: Norton, 1994.

Silverstein, Michael. *Treasure Hunt: Inside the Mind of the New Consumer*. New York: Portfolio, 2006.

Silvester, Trevor. *WordWeaving: The Science of Suggestion*. Cambs, England: Quest, 2003.

————. *WordWeaving*. Vol. 2, *The Question Is the Answer*. Cambs, England: Quest, 2006.

Simmons, Annette. *The Story Factor: Inspiration, Influence, and Persuasion through the Art of Storytelling*. Cambridge, MA: Perseus, 2001.

Smith, P. R. *Marketing Communications: An Integrated Approach*. London: Kogan Page, 2004.

Snyder, Edward. *Hypnotic Poetry: A Study of Trance-Inducing Technique in Certain Poems and Its Literary Significance*. Philadelphia: University of Pennsylvania Press, 1924.

Sommer, Elyse. *As One Mad with Wine and Other Similes*. New York: Visible Ink, 1991.

Stafford, Tom, and Matt Webb. *Mind Hacks: Tips & Tools for Using Your Brain*. Sebastopol, CA: O'Reilly Media, 2005.

Stevenson, Michael. *Learn Hypnosis . . . Now! The Easiest Way to Learn Hypnosis*. Laguna Hills, CA: Liquid Mirror Enterprises, 2005.

St. James, Martin. *Sleep You Bastard! The True Misadventures of the World's Greatest Hypnotist*. Melbourne, Australia: Spellbound Promotions, 1993.

Straus, Roger. *Creative Self-Hypnosis*. Lincoln, NE: iUniverse, 2000.

Streeter, Michael. *Hypnosis: Secrets of the Mind*. Hauppauge, N.Y.: Barron's, 2004.

Sugarman, Joe. *Advertising Secrets of the Written Word*. Las Vegas, NV: DelStar, 1998.

————. *Triggers: 30 Sales Tools You Can Use to Control the Mind of Your Prospect to Motivate, Influence and Persuade.* Las Vegas, NV: DelStar, 1999.

Sweet, Robert Burdette. *Writing Towards Wisdom: The Writer as Shaman.* Carmichael, CA: Helios House, 1990.

Thompson, Peter. *Persuading Aristotle: The Timeless Art of Persuasion in Business, Negotiation and the Media.* New South Wales, Australia: Allen & Unwin, 1998.

Underhill, Paco. *Why We Buy: The Science of Shopping.* New York: Simon & Schuster, 1999.

Vitale, Joe. *The AMA Complete Guide to Small Business Advertising.* Lincolnwood, IL: NTC Business Books, 1995.

————. *The Attractor Factor: 5 Easy Steps for Creating Wealth (or Anything Else) from the Inside Out.* Hoboken, NJ: John Wiley & Sons, 2005.

————. *Hypnotic Writing.* Hoboken, NJ: John Wiley & Sons, 2006.

————. *Life's Missing Instruction Manual: The Guidebook You Should Have Been Given at Birth.* Hoboken, NJ: John Wiley & Sons, 2006.

————. *The Seven Lost Secrets of Success.* New ed. Hampton Roads, VA: Morgan James, 2005.

————. *There's a Customer Born Every Minute: P. T. Barnum's 10 Rings of Power for Fame, Fortune and Building an Empire.* Hoboken, NJ: John Wiley & Sons, 2006.

————. *Turbocharge Your Writing.* Houston, TX: Awareness Publications, 1992.

————. *Zen and the Art of Writing.* Costa Mesa, CA: Westcliff, 1984.

Vitale, Joe, and Bill Hibbler. *Meet and Grow Rich.* Hoboken, NJ: John Wiley & Sons, 2006.

Vitale, Joe, and I. Len. *Zero Limits.* Hoboken, NJ: John Wiley & Sons (in press).

Vitale, Joe, and Jo Han Mok. *The E-Code.* Hoboken, NJ: John Wiley & Sons, 2005.

Vogele, Siegfried. *Handbook of Direct Mail: The Dialogue Method of Direct Written Sales Communication.* Upper Saddle River, NJ: Prentice-Hall, 1992.

Wallas, Lee. *Stories for the Third Ear: Using Hypnotic Fables in Psychotherapy.* New York: Norton, 1985.

Walsh, Brian. *Unleashing Your Brilliance.* Victoria, BC, Canada: Walsh Seminars, 2005.

Warren, Blair. *Forbidden Keys to Persuasion.* San Antonio, TX: Warren Productions, 2003.

Waterfield, Robin. *Hidden Depths: The Story of Hypnosis.* New York: Macmillan, 2002.

Wertime, Kent. *Building Brands and Believers: How to Connect with Consumers Using Archetypes.* Hoboken, NJ: John Wiley & Sons, 2002.

Wheeler, Elmer. *How to Tap Your Hidden Sources of Energy.* Englewood Cliffs, NJ: Prentice-Hall, 1962.

———. *Selling Dangerously.* Englewood Cliffs, NJ: Prentice-Hall, 1956.

———. *Sizzlemanship: New Tested Selling Sentences.* Englewood Cliffs, NJ: Prentice-Hall, 1941.

———. *Tested Salesmanship.* Dallas, TX: Elmer Wheeler Sales Training Institute, 1948.

———. *Tested Sentences That Sell.* Englewood Cliffs, NJ: Prentice-Hall, 1937.

———. *Word Magic.* Englewood Cliffs, NJ: Prentice-Hall, 1939.

Wilber, Ken. *A Brief History of Everything.* Boston: Shambhala, 2000.

Williams, Roy. *Secret Formulas of the Wizard of Ads.* Austin, TX: Bard Press, 1999.

Wind, Jerry, and Colin Crook. *The Power of Impossible Thinking.* Upper Saddle River, NJ: Wharton School Publishing, 2005.

Wolinsky, Stephen. *Trances People Live: Healing Approaches in Quantum Psychology.* Falls Village, CT: Bramble, 1991.

Zaltman, Gerald. *How Customers Think: Essential Insights into the Mind of the Market*. Boston: Harvard Business School Press, 2003.

Zarren, Jordan. *Brief Cognitive Hypnosis*. New York: Springer, 2002.

Zeig, Jeffrey. *Experiencing Erickson: An Introduction to the Man and His Work*. Bristol, PA: Brunner/Mazel, 1985.

———. *The Letters of Milton H. Erickson*. Phoenix, AZ: Zeig, Tucker & Theisen Publishers, 2000.

About Dr. Joe Vitale

D r. Joe Vitale is president of Hypnotic Marketing, Inc., an Internet marketing firm. He is the author of way too many books to list here, including the #1 best-selling books *The Attractor Factor: 5 Easy Steps for Creating Wealth (or Anything Else) from the Inside Out* and *Life's Missing Instruction Manual: The Guidebook You Should Have Been Given at Birth*, and the best-selling Nightingale-Conant audioprogram, *The Power of Outrageous Marketing*.

His latest books include *Hypnotic Writing*, *There's a Customer Born Every Minute*, *Meet and Grow Rich* (with Bill Hibbler), *The Greatest Money-Making Secret in History*, *Adventures Within*, *The Seven Lost Secrets of Success*, *The Successful Coach* (with Terri Levine and Larina Kase), and *The E-Code* (with Jo Han Mok). His next book will be *Zero Limits* (with I. Len).

He also created a software program to help you write sales letters, ads, news releases, speeches, and even entire books using his hypnotic writing and Buying Trances methods. You can learn more about it at www.hypnoticwritingwizard.com.

You can sign up to receive Dr. Vitale's free monthly e-newsletter, "News You Can Use," at his main web site at www.mrfire.com.

His corporate site is at www.hypnoticmarketingInc.com.

Index